CELEBRATING
Relationships

Also by Sirshree

* Spiritual Masterpieces- Self Realisation books for serious seekers *

The Secret of Awakening
Secret of the Third Side of the Coin : Unravelling Missing Links in Spirituality
100% Karma : Learn the Art of Conscious Karma that Liberates
100% Wisdom:Wisdom that leads you to experience and be established in your true nature
You are Meditation : Discover Peace and Bliss Within
Essence of Devotion : From Devotee to Divinity
Dip into Oneness : Beyond Knower, Known and Knowing
The Unshaken Mind : Discovering the Purpose, Power and Potential of your mind
The Supreme Quest : Your search for the Truth ends there where you are
The Greatest Freedom : Discover the key to an Awakened Living
Seek Forfiveness & be Free : Liberation from Karmic Bondage
Passwords to a Happy Life : The Art of Being Happy in all Situaltion
The Light of Grace : Why Guru, God, Grace and You are one
Why Jesus Didn't Work A Miracle During Crucifixion
Secrets of Shiva

* Self Help Treasures - Self Development books for success seekers *

The Source of Health: The Key to Perfect Health Discovery
Inner Ninety Hidden Infinity : How to build your book of values
Inner 90 for Youth : The secret of reaching and staying at the peak of success
The Source for Youth : You have the power to change your life
Inner Magic : The Power of self-talk
The Five Supreme Secrets of Life : Unveiling the Ways to Attain Wealth, Love and God
Freedom from Failure : 7 Spiritual Secrets that Transform Failure into a Blessing
You are Not Lazy : A story of shifting from Laziness to Success
Freedom From Fear, Worry, Anger : How to be cool, calm and courageous
Mastering the Art of Decision Making : How to Make the Highest Choice
Complete Parenting : How to raise your child with grace

New Age Nuggets - Practical books on applied spirituality and self help

The Source : Power of Happy Thoughts
Secret of Happiness : Instant Happiness - Here and Now!
Excuse me God... : Fulfilling your wishes through the Power of Prayer and Seed of Faith
Help God to Help You : Whatever you do, do it with a smile
Ultimate Purpose of Success: Achieving Success in all five aspects of life
Celebrating Relationships : Bringing Love, Life, Laughter in Your Relations
Everything is a Game of Beliefs : Understanding is the Whole Thing
Detachment From Attachment : Gift of Freedom From Suffering
Emotional Freedom Through Spiritual Wisdom
The Miracle Mind : How to master your mind before it masters you
The Power of Present : Experience the Joy of the Now

* Profound Parables - Fiction books containing profound truths *

Beyond Life : Conversations on Life After Death
The Source @ Work : A Story of Inspiration from Jeeodee
The One Above : What if God was your neighbour?
The Warrior's Mirror : The Path To Peace
Master of Siddhartha: Revealing the Truth of Life and After-life
Put Stress to Rest : Utilizing Stress to Make Progress

CELEBRATING
Relationships

Bring Love, Life, Laughter in Your Relations

Celebrating Relationships
By Tejgyan Global Foundation
Inspired by Sirshree Tejparkhi

Copyright © Tejgyan Global Foundation
All Rights Reserved 2009

Tejgyan Global Foundation is a charitable organization
with its headquarters in Pune, India.

ISBN : 978-81-8415-414-6

Published by WOW Publishings Pvt. Ltd., India

Third Edition published in January 2016

First Reprint published in October 2016

Second Reprint published in September 2020

Printed and bound by Trinity Academy, Pune, INDIA

Copyrights are reserved with Tejgyan Global Foundation and publishing rights are vested exclusively with WOW Publishings Pvt. Ltd. This book is sold subject to the condition that it shall not by way of trade or otherwise, be lent, resold, hired out, or otherwise circulated without the publisher's prior written consent in any form of binding or cover other than that in which it is published and without a similar condition including this condition being imposed on the subsequent purchaser and without limiting the rights under copyright reserved above, no part of this publication may be reproduced, stored in or introduced into a retrieval system, or transmitted, in any form, or by any means, electronic, mechanical, photocopying, recording or otherwise, without the prior written permission of both the copyright owner and the above-mentioned publisher of this book. Any person who does any unauthorized act in relation to this publication may be liable to criminal prosecution and civil claims for damages.

Although the author and publisher have made every effort to ensure accuracy of content in this book, they hereby disclaim any liability to any party for any loss, damage, or disruption caused by errors or omissions, resulting from negligence, accident, or any other cause. Readers are advised to take full responsibility to exercise discretion in understanding and applying the content of this book.

CONTENTS

	Preface: Transform Your Relationships into a Celebration	7

Section I : Importance of Relationships and Message of Love — 13

1.	Priceless Gift of Our Ancestors for Maintaining Relationships	15
2.	A Bigger Goal Demands More Well-Wishers	20
3.	Learning to Live The Right Way	25

Section II : How to Remove Negativity from Relationships — 29

4.	What There Must Be in Relationships	31
5.	What There Must Not Be in Relationships	34
6.	How to Save Your Family Tree From Being Cut Down	38
7.	How to Fill The Love Bank Of Your Family	42
8.	How to Keep Love Alive in Relationships	48
9.	How To Avoid the Sword of Words in Relationships	52
10.	How Can An Understanding Family Become A Happy Family	55
11.	To Improve Relationships, First Improve Yourself	58

Section III : How to Communicate in Relationships in the Right Manner — 61

12.	Choose Words That Bring Warmth in Relations	63
13.	Stop Miscommunication in Relationships	65
14.	Neither Think Aloud Nor Remain Silent	69
15.	How to Make Your Relationships Complete	73

Section IV : How to Strengthen Relationships In The Family		77
16.	Husband-Wife and Children	79
17.	Get Together and Make Plans for Your Life	83
18.	How to Build Three Higher Platforms for Communication in the Family	85
19.	How to Make Your Home a Heaven	96
Section V : Transform Yourself, Others, and the World		99
20.	Magical Step 1: We Become What We Focus On	101
21.	Magical Step 2: Appreciate Generously	109
22.	Magical Step 3: Become a Good News Reporter	119
Section VI : Break Down Walls and Connect with People, Guru and God		125
23.	How to Break the Walls Between Relationships - 1	127
24.	How to Break the Walls Between Relationships - 2	133
25.	How to Break the Walls Between Relationships - 3	138
26.	Learn the Art of Forgiving and Forgetting	142
27.	Connection between Relations and Thoughts	148
28.	How to Build Good Relations with People	156
29.	Build a Relationship That Will Transform You	160
30.	How to Build a Relationship with God	166
	Epilogue: The Golden Rule	169
	APPENDIX	175

Preface

*Illuminate your relationships with a new light
that reveals the underlying oneness and common goal.*

Transform Your Relationships into a Celebration

With good wishes in your mind, and a new book in your hands, you may well hope to receive a new light. Experience a glimpse of this new light in your life right now with the following scenario.

Have you ever wondered what would happen if all the fingers of your hand were the same? If all were equal in size and shape? How would you work, write, or eat? Imagine yourself performing your normal activities with such a hand. Would it be easy and comfortable? Or would it be the opposite?

You are right. A hand with equal fingers would be quite a problem. Even your simple daily activities could only be carried out with difficulty because of the awkward movements of your hands. Whether you were cooking, driving, typing, washing, or anything else, you would have lots of problems. But what is the reason? Why couldn't your fingers, which are only demanding equality, help you with your activities?

In this example, none of your fingers are fatter or thinner, shorter or taller, than the others. So what is the problem? Perhaps, through this illustration, you may have already understood a few important things about life.

The objective of this book is to illuminate your relationships with a new light. And the example above, about different fingers of the hand, may make things clearer. Fingers symbolize our various relationships. Any work gets done perfectly when our fingers are unequal. If they became equal, they would lose their beauty and functionality. A home may have a certain number of members, who may be short or tall, fat or thin, quiet or boisterous, successful or unsuccessful. But these differences do not make any one individual inferior or superior to the others. In fact, these differences enable each to help one another. All they need is a bright torch of understanding to help them complete their journey and reach the destination. This light will reveal their oneness, as one single hand, and enable them to see their common goal.

An ignorant person may get impressed by the thumb and would want to see all his fingers so sturdy and strong. At other times, he may be impressed by his middle finger, and would prefer to see all his fingers long. Sometimes, he may even think, "Since my right hand is so useful, why can't I have the thumb of my left hand on my right hand? Then, I can really achieve something great and impress the world." This desire leads to a lifelong struggle for him. However, once he receives the torch of understanding in his hands, from that day he allows all the fingers of his hand to be as they are.

This feeling of acceptance feels like a new light. When he could not accept it, there were conflicts and dissatisfactions in his life. The day he recognized the beauty of nature and the unity behind its diversity, he shed all his resistance and non-acceptance. Now, he accepts all his fingers and their positions on the hand.

If your middle finger starts considering itself to be a *Brahmin* (the priestly highest rank in the ancient Hindu caste system), and the thumb a *Kshatriya* (warrior class), then won't they be able to work together as a team? If the index finger considers itself to be a *Vaishya* (trader or merchant class) and the little finger a *Shudra* (lowest working class), then together can't they lift a broom? In fact, they can not only lift the broom, but also sweep the dirt of separatism clean. Such an act of camaraderie can help to break all restrictive beliefs in religion, caste, and creed.

While sweeping and collecting dust from the floor, one of the fingers has to be on the lower side. Only then can cleaning taking place. Thus, while collecting dust, if the little finger remains on the lowest side facing the floor, then this is its greatness, not its weakness. If one person in the family is responsible for maintaining cleanliness, then someone else looks after the family's safety and security. If someone earns money for feeding the family, then someone else plans for its future. Every member is working for the same family. Carrying the torch of love and understanding, all the members will stay happy. The day this torch extinguishes, each one will start thinking only about oneself and believe they are superior. Words like Brahmin, Shudra, Kshatriya, and Vaishya, which were created to facilitate division of work, will become a noose around the neck. People will become troublesome and try to defeat each other in their struggle for superiority. To prevent such a situation from arising, we must understand why the caste system was made in the first place. Every finger has a different role. This is each finger's beauty, not its weakness. Small, big, or fat; when these fingers beat together on a drum, they produce wonderful music, which makes one dance with joy. Isn't this a miracle of nature? Understand this arrangement made by nature and assimilate it into your life. Then see your relationships glow with a warm new spirit.

You are learning the art of improving relationships from this analogy of a hand. You are learning to accept people as they are, because only after such acceptance can you appreciate the delightfulness in your relationships. Allow each finger to be as it is. Give time and space to allow every relationship to open and blossom. Learn to view every relationship in a new light and fill each with the color of supreme love.

Whenever you feel that you are getting irritated by your relatives, ask yourself, "What exactly is happening here? Do I know the entire picture (goal) of the master artist (God) about why am I here on Earth? If I believe I do know the entire picture, then what is it I know?" Upon asking yourself these questions, you will find that all your irritation stops at once. You will come to know that this special arrangement of relationships has been made on Earth for making your mind pure, loving, and steadfast.

The Earth is a school in which you have to always remain aware and ready to learn your lessons. You have been given several relatives, who create a special environment around you. You should be happy for this exceptional arrangement provided to you. The interactions within the family help to make your mind pure and firm. You have come to Earth to work on your mind. If you do so, the self-expression that will take place through you will be extraordinary. You will become instrumental for others to also attain happiness, love, and fulfillment. You will then be able to stay happy even while facing stress in relationships.

When everything in the family is going really well and according to your mind's wishes, your mind isn't getting the necessary training to deal with difficulties. When you can remain happy, despite some adversity within the family, then you are gaining the understanding that is necessary in your relationships.

You must check in every situation whether you are utilizing and deriving benefit from the arrangement that has been provided to you on Earth or whether it is making you feel miserable. If you can make your relationships a medium for learning higher lessons, then you will never feel troubled by them. This is because you need to be amidst these relationships to achieve your ultimate goal.

If you feel irritated by relationships, in fact this is an answer to your own prayers. Your inner desire or prayer was to be free from anger; therefore, stressful situations in your relationships have been created for you by nature. When you actually understand this, you will feel like laughing at yourself. You will then be liberated from both anger and tension in your relationships.

The World is an Arrangement for Love and Faith

This world is an arrangement made for us, a playground for practice, where we can train ourselves in understanding the Truth. Only after attaining the purpose for which mankind has come to Earth do we realize: "Had I not attained this purpose, I would have lost the greatest happiness of my life." This world has been made for mankind to achieve the whole and sole goal of life, that is, Self-Realization. After attaining Self-Realization, we need to get established in that state and express the qualities of the Self – love, bliss, faith, purity, steadfastness, courage, etc. Those who are clear about this goal understand what death is and what life after death is; thus they also understand the drama that is being enacted on Earth. For this reason, they do not become entangled in this drama. Instead, they watch the drama without getting caught up in it. They enjoy it and also become instrumental in spreading happiness. In doing this, they develop two qualities – supreme faith and supreme love – here on Earth.

Only if we can have faith in one another, and give love, can real happiness emerge from our hearts. Even a little bit of faith and love gives rise to so much happiness. Just think how much happiness there would be when complete love and faith that lie dormant within us are awakened and released to the world! Arrangements for this have been provided on this Earth, so that you can get at least a taste of this happiness. You sometimes do get a taste, but then forget your real goal by becoming involved in other things. Then you need to be reminded: "It is for releasing supreme love and faith that you are born on Earth, through which the mind becomes pure, loving, and steadfast."

The family into which you were born in this world is a custom-made arrangement especially for you. You have to practice in this family in order to attain your real goal. Various relations have been given to you to facilitate the awakening of supreme love and faith within you. This book is a 30-day self-retreat that elaborates on ways to benefit from this arrangement.

This is not merely a book but also a family retreat. You are not only a reader of this book, but also the facilitator and organizer of this retreat for your family. Congratulations for participating in this retreat. Do keep the torch of understanding burning bright so that you never forget the actual purpose of relationships. Then your relationships won't be just a formality, a responsibility, or a burden… but a celebration!

–Sirshree

HOW TO GET THE MAXIMUM FROM THIS FAMILY RETREAT

1. This book is a self-retreat. This means you can read one chapter a day and contemplate it in depth. This will help you apply the teachings in your own life and you will see the results in your relationships.

2. If a rift has occurred in any of your relationships, for example, with your mother, father, sister, brother, friend, neighbor, or anyone else, then read the first three chapters of *Section VI* of this book first. This will immediately break all the walls that exist in your relationships (Day 23 – 25).

3. If you want to learn the art of human relations, if you want to be recognized as a talented and capable person in society, and if you want to be successful, then read *Section V* of this book first. The three-step magical formula will certainly help you in reaching your goal (Day 20 – 22).

4. If you want to get rid of problems in your relationships, read *Section II* of this book on what should exist in relations and what should not (Day 4 – 11).

5. In order to stop wrong communication in relationships, read *Section III* of this book, which elaborates the art of right communication and how to achieve completeness in communications (Day 12 – 15).

6. If you want to strengthen the foundation of your family ties and make your home blissful, read *Section IV* of this book (Day 16 – 19).

7. If you harbor hatred towards someone or if someone harbors hatred towards you, then you should read *Section VI*, 'Learn the Art of Forgiving and Forgetting' (Day 26).

8. To understand the connection between thoughts and relationships and the rule of life, and to know how to move ahead in relationships, read *Section VI*. This is a must read for everyone (Day 27).

Section I

IMPORTANCE OF RELATIONSHIPS AND MESSAGE OF LOVE

1

*Fill the world of your relationships
with the fragrance of faith and the potion of love.*

PRICELESS GIFT OF OUR ANCESTORS FOR MAINTAINING RELATIONSHIPS

Message of love and the purpose of festivals

"*Every major success in the world can be achieved only with the support of relatives and friends.*" Do you agree with this thought? If yes, then this book will help you earn the necessary support and cooperation of people. If you disagree, then you can skip this chapter and proceed to read the rest of the book. Thereafter, you can return to this chapter.

To escape the pitfalls of failure, it is extremely important to bring about an improvement in our relationships. Those who do not understand the importance of relationships do not possess the art of human relations and can never achieve major success in life. Therefore, to maintain all your relationships and to strengthen them, it is important to undertake this self-retreat over a month. You can complete this retreat earlier, but by reading one chapter each day and contemplating it in depth, you can apply these teachings progressively in your own life.

Through this study you will learn how to behave with people, how to talk with them, how to work with them, how to plan your life together with real love, and how to bring all these suggestions into practice and see your relationships in a new light.

Two methods have been traditionally used for improving relations:

One is by using force and the other is by using love and patience.

For ages, man's behavior has been influenced by the use of force, just like the law of the jungle. But now the time has come to make a loving effort to improve our relations, and to make the time to contemplate this so as to bring about the progress of mankind. We must all learn how to interact with others, how to achieve things from others, how to help others, and how we can contribute to inspiring others.

Love and Efforts of our Ancestors

In order to fulfil our main purpose of being born on Earth (which you have learned in the preface) and to derive maximum benefit from our relationships, our wise ancestors – free from dogma and ignorance – designed certain festivals. These festivals were devised as a pretext to improve relationships and to remind us how with love we should bond with friends, relatives, and all others. Festivals represent a means to bring about harmony and warmth in relations, by removing personal ego and making the mind loving.

Our ancestors created many customs with considerable thought, such as which foods should be eaten in which season to maintain good health, and which rituals should be performed to enhance particular relationships. Certain rituals and certain foods were associated with particular festivals, so that we might gain good health as well as achieve our main purpose on Earth. If we gain only physical health while our intellect remains unhealthy, we will never attain complete health. With the aid of festivals, the dirt and dust which has accumulated on the intellect, as well as on relationships, can be wiped clean.

Those with impure minds and unhappy relationships need a soap to cleanse the mind of all the dirt that has collected in it. Festivals provide us with that soap (knowledge and opportunity) to purify our mind. Festivals give the message of surrendering the mind. Do not celebrate festivals as mere customs, but as celebrations that can bring new light into relationships and enable us to attain total health.

An individual who recognizes the significance of health will always want to feel fit and healthy in every respect. Thinking may arise along such lines as: "I am free from all major ailments, so why should I have minor problems? I have overcome many bad habits, so why should I still have this remaining wrong habit? Why do I sometimes feel angry on seeing this particular person when I feel love with others? Why has only this relationship remained incomplete? How can I bring completeness into this relationship as well?"

Anyone who wants to develop or maintain good health will not want sickness in any facet of life. The objective must be to eliminate those unwanted or inappropriate relationships which cause sickness or discomfort and replace them only with love.

Man's intellect, body, mind, and relationships are unhealthy. This is why several days in every year have been allocated by our predecessors to become festivals that can restore our health. Thus, festivals are a priceless gift to us from our forefathers.

Various Festivals and Special Days

Every major festival, everywhere in the world, invariably brings people together. If you consider the main festivals in every religion, for example, Diwali, Eid, or Christmas, you will notice that these festivals not only bring us closer to each other, but also closer to God. What an excellent arrangement! How would our lives be without these festivals?!

In addition, some special days are celebrated as a tribute to particular relationships. On these special days we are intended to contemplate that particular relationship in depth. For example, Mother's Day is to honor our mom and to express our gratitude for all the hardships she has faced in raising us. Though we live with our mother for many years, most of us hardly ever thank her for what she has done for us. We take her for granted. But the truth is, our lives would be so much harder without our mother. So this day becomes an opportunity to convey our love and enrich this truly divine relationship.

Father's Day is celebrated to honor our dad and to thank him for being the backbone of our life. It is a good day to remove any obstacles in the relationship and to open up. If we have never hugged our father, this is our chance to get closer to him. It is also a good opportunity to buy him a gift for a change, especially when it's usually the father who provides everything for the family.

On Grandparents' Day, we are more sensitive towards our grandparents and give them all our love and respect. Children's Day is to celebrate childhood and to honor children and minors. Friendship Day is celebrated to renew and reinforce old friendships as well as to make new ones. *Raksha Bandhan* is celebrated in India to strengthen the relationship between brothers and sisters. On *Karva Chauth,* which can also be called Husband's Day, the wife observes a fast for the well-being and long life of her husband. *Guru Poornima* is celebrated to honor our spiritual guru and get back on track if we have strayed away from the path of Truth. Teacher's Day is celebrated to honor all teachers, and this day also presents us a chance to overcome any problems that may exist between teachers and students. Doctor's Day is for us to express our gratitude to our doctors for helping us maintain good health. Other days, such as World Animal Day, Environment Day, and so on, are also celebrated to create awareness and fortify our relationship with the environment around us.

Certain festivals have been designed for improving all relationships at once. The festival of *Makar Sankranti,* celebrated in some parts of India, is one such festival. Certain rituals involving the daughter-in-law, mother-in-law, father-in-law, brother-in-law, sister-in-law, brother, sister, and all other relations are performed. This helps them all to get closer and bring warmth into their relationships. People visit each other and exchange sweets. The young touch the elders' feet as a mark of respect, while the elders give the young their blessings. Notably, on this day the elders correctly respect the youth, as one should respect the rising sun. Youth need the acknowledgment of respect, whereas elders are not in such need since through their lives they have already gained wisdom. (In fact, 'elder' is a term only used for those who have gained wisdom.) Elders understand the strong desire in young minds to seek attention of others and the kind of mistakes they can make in fulfilling this desire.

Thus, teenagers must get respect from elders, but they must also seek blessings from the elders in order to subjugate their egos. Unfortunately, the opposite generally happens, with teenagers being constantly instructed instead of respected. *"Do this, do that... sit like this, stand like that... say this, don't say that... behave this way with guests... get on with your study not your games!"* Too often, they only get orders. No wonder so-called elders frequently consider teenagers to be 'out of order'. In this case, 'out of order' means they believe they are 'out of discipline'.

We should understand the new thinking of our new era and show a new light to our youth. The need of the times is to realize the inherent purpose of all festivals for relationships, and to bring this knowledge into action in the right manner. Our ancestors devised these amazing practices to renew relationships and to help maintain them. If these practices presently seem in vain, then we need to light the torch of understanding and start afresh. Come, let us all try to light this torch together and celebrate our relationships in this new light.

In the next chapter, we shall discover the connection between our festivals, our goal, and our relationships.

2

*Those who cannot bow in relationships
can never attain love, happiness, or success.*

A Bigger Goal Demands More Well-Wishers

People aren't as bad as we think

When you seek people's blessing and bow before them with love and understanding, they will become your well-wishers. You will need many well-wishers to attain your goal in life. If you cannot bow before anyone because of your ego and haughtiness, no one will support you.

A person who is able and accustomed to receive blessings from others will be at ease meeting and mingling with people. Such a person will give others respect and receive their blessings and support in return. Therefore, if your goal in life is big, you will need to establish many well-wishers for yourself. The bigger your goal, the more supporters and helpful hands you will need.

Dahi-handi is an Indian festival that follows the anniversary of Lord Krishna's birth. In this festival, a pot of curd is suspended from a rope at a great height. A human pyramid is then formed so that one person can climb to the top and reach the elusive pot. Anyone aiming for the loftiest *dahi-handi* (the highest goal) requires the support of a large number of people. The higher the pot, or goal, the greater the number of supportive hands that are needed.

In life, like the human pyramid, many people will stand at the bottom offering their combined strength. Above them will stand more supporters, and above them, yet more. With this support in place, an individual can climb to the top on the shoulders of others, and reach the desired goal. Then finally, upon reaching the goal, everyone who gave support becomes a partner in that goal. This principle is clear and the conclusion must be that only with the support of many others can one succeed in one's endeavors.

If your goal is small, then you will need the support and blessings of only a few people. If your goal is big, then you will need the support of as many people as possible. From the example of *Dahi-handi*, you can learn the secrets of achieving success by bringing harmony into your relationships.

To fully benefit from this secret, always see virtues in people, because the quality on which you focus starts growing inside you as well. To make progress in your life, learn to live in harmony with everyone, and focus on their virtues. You will find the mind finds it easier to bend when acknowledging the virtues in others. Those who do not know how to concede to others will never achieve any major success.

It is true that initially the mind may not feel inclined to bow before another. The rigidity of our mind can make this seem impossible. But if we give up our resistance, we will find we are well-received, and we will be blessed by the person before whom we bow. As a result, outlooks shift, and each feels that the other is not as bad as perhaps assumed.

People will often resist coming face to face with each other. Yet, how can they know one another until they do? In many relationships, people do not even want to see each other, and if they happen to do so, they turn their face and walk away. When relations turn bitter, even those living in the same house can arrange their timings to avoid one another.

Festivals can be a salvation for such poor relationships. A festival arrives and rituals need to be performed between people according to the custom. This may involve sharing special meals or performing some activities together, giving gifts or sweets to each other, applying colors to one another, and so on. These rituals and customs play an important part in mitigating the distance between the hearts of people.

People gather together on these days, and as they mix, love between them can blossom. They give and receive blessings, and learn that others are not as bad as they may have thought. Without the aid of such harmonizing events, we can form wrong notions in our minds. We look at people around us through prejudiced glasses. Since we feel uncomfortable about changing our glasses and our biased beliefs, we prefer to continue thinking that our prejudices are right.

See a new person in a new light

Over time, every individual undergoes some changes. Yet, whenever we meet people, we always see them in the same light. Consider a person who was once ill-natured. Should we think the same about that person on meeting them after many years? No. We don't know what experiences they have been through, how many influential books they might have read, or how many transforming people they have encountered. Any of life's experiences may have changed them and this should be our perspective. Unfortunately, no one is ready to think that other people may have changed. We always look at people with the same old impressions that are imprinted in our mind. We refuse to see anything other than the old and stale. We live our life viewing from the past and never see people in the present, as they are. It is time we challenged our preconceived notions and began to look for the fresh and the new.

Let the mother-in-law and daughter-in-law enact with awareness

On the day of the festival *Sankranti*, there is a custom that the mother-in-law should deliberately become upset with her daughter-in-law and leave for the neighbor's house. The daughter-in-law then goes to her and feigns trying to please her, and requests her to come back. But the mother-in-law stubbornly rejects the appeal and replies, "Go away, I shan't return." The daughter-in-law now apologizes with sincerity and says, "In future, I will be careful not to make mistakes. Please come back to us." The mother-in-law is thus appeased, and together they duly return to their home.

This drama was purposely created to undo any antagonisms between mother-in-law and daughter-in-law and to bring back warmth and love in their relationship. Both are aware they are acting a part and all is light-hearted fun. But in the process they also develop an awareness about their quarrels. This is called 'negative practice with awareness'. The benefit of this custom is that when the next time, they actually argue over some issue, they will recall the dialogue they spoke during *Sankranti*. In this way, awareness increases and the argument will cease. It is only due to this festival that the participants have the opportunity to use this technique to raise their awareness and make their relations better.

If someone has a habit of biting nails and wants to get rid of the habit, tell them: "Try biting your nails consciously. Be aware the moment your hand goes to your mouth and you start biting your nails." Ask them to practice this for a while. Soon, the result will be that when their hand goes to their mouth, they will become spontaneously aware of this habit. The hand will go down, and the habit will be stopped, perhaps permanently.

If we practice awareness in this way, we can put an end to any bad habit. When we work with awareness, whatever is bad stops, and the good begins to happen. By working with awareness, we are able to see what we are doing in the present moment. What are the consequences of this feeling, thought, word or action? If a smoker starts smoking with awareness, he will soon realize what he is actually doing. He will ask himself: "How can I indulge in such foolishness – holding and inhaling from a roll of burning paper in my mouth, which can cause serious diseases and a miserable death?" Continuing to smoke with awareness will soon end the smoking habit.

Smile please

Contemplation is a must if you want to maintain awareness in your relationships. Many festivals have been created, not just in India but in countries throughout the world. The frequency of such festivals can enable us to contemplate regularly. Festivals encourage us to act consciously together. They help to make our day-to-day relations pleasant by reminding us how to interact gently with each other. With this experience, there should be no need to ask anyone to "please behave politely."

The fact that we need to ask others to be polite indicates that we have forgotten how to interact with each other. The reason for the sign reading 'Smile Please' is that we have forgotten to smile or there is a possibility that we may forget to smile. It is important to remind those with sullen faces to smile and to express love. And why are laughter clubs now springing up? Because people have forgotten to laugh.

Giving respect and receiving blessings is becoming rare in relationships today. There is the possibility of forgetting them altogether. May such negative possibilities in relationships perish and positive ones blossom into reality. This is the new light. To ignite it, we must learn the right way to live life.

3

Develop the habit of keeping things in a proper way at the proper place, and your relationships too will start falling into place.

LEARNING TO LIVE THE RIGHT WAY
I am wonderful and so are you

It is imperative to know how to live life the right way and how to filter out hatred from the essence of love. To know how to live life the right way is to know how to keep our belongings and our thoughts in the right place. Not everyone keeps things in order.

The first rule of good house-keeping is: 'A place for everything and everything in its place.' Those who follow this rule know exactly where each object should go and put everything in its appropriate location. Those who do not know this rule tend to throw things here, there, and everywhere. What happens with such people? They lose valuable time trying to find things they need. But more than this, such a lifestyle results in the development of the bad habit of carelessness. Those who handle objects carelessly, will handle their relationships carelessly too. Furthermore, when thinking about any subject, they do that in the same careless manner. Due to lack of structure in their thinking, their thoughts run haywire without direction. Without sequence or depth to their thinking, solutions to problems can't be found. With any thought barging randomly into their mind, they get so lost in thoughts that they may not only cause harm to themselves but also to others.

If you do not keep outer things in order, it affects your inner world too. This means that anything you do externally has a similar effect within you. If you live carelessly on the outside, then everything inside you will also become disorderly. Hence, you should develop the habit of keeping everything properly in order. When you cultivate this habit of orderliness, you will see its impact in every aspect of your life. All your relationships will fall into place. Everything in your life will happen on time. Otherwise, everything will remain hanging half done, even your ultimate success.

While on their deathbed, people who have led disorderly lives and never finished anything on time feel that they have lived just for namesake. They feel as if there was no purpose to their life and that they failed to consider the questions: "Why was I born? How should I make use of this life?"

Learn the art of mending relationships

To improve relationships, one must do everything with awareness. Whatever you do, ask yourself, "What is my purpose behind doing this? Is that purpose being fulfilled?" The purpose of this book is to mend our relationships, which can be done by following the Golden Rule and other methods described later in this book. After mending, our mutual relationships are repaired into ones of love and respect. Without such mending, our viewpoint in most relationships is usually: "I am right, you are wrong." Though there are some people who suffer from inferiority, who say, "You are right, I am wrong." Such people always believe others are better than themselves; that others act better, think better, and are more successful. But whether one considers oneself superior or inferior, when their understanding increases, they say: "I am right, and so are you." They recognize that both are correct, in their own ways, from their own points of view. Thereafter, both are able to listen to each other patiently, without criticism of one another.

After this state, there comes a further state in which they can feel "I am wonderful, and so are you." Now, they start interacting happily with each other. When everything is wonderful, then everyone is right. To attain such understanding, and to progress from being 'right' to being 'wonderful', each of us need to understand the depth of our relationships and then work on enhancing them. Subsequently, everyone will be able to mix with each other and work together easily. Quarrelling will be consigned to the past.

An angry man gets into clashes with his family and other people every day. One day, on the special occasion of a festival, he is warned in advance, "Today, you must not fight at all or it is believed that you'll keep fighting throughout the year." When he is given this thought, he decides firmly, "Today, I won't fight or argue at all. I can follow this rule at least for today. After all, it's just for one day and not for my whole life." What happens during this day is that he gets a welcome taste of not fighting or being in dispute. Instead, he experiences tranquility and self-control. He then starts thinking, "If I can last one day without quarreling, then why can't I do this every day?" He has discovered he likes the silence, peace, and love he has experienced and wants to live this way all his life. In this manner, a single resolution can become a huge opportunity for strengthening the foundation of relationships.

During a particular festival, a dish is prepared that uses a mix of many vegetables. Why would this ritual have been created? Because many people say, "I don't like this particular vegetable and there's no way I'd eat it, even if you tried to force me." They need to be persuaded that the first time they tried this vegetable the situation was different. Perhaps their stomach was already upset, or the food wasn't fresh. Today is a different day, so they should at least try the vegetable one more time.

Under the pretext of this festival, people experiment by trying to eat those vegetables that previously they could not. This kind of experiment is essential. Children willingly experiment in most things but, most of the time, the older generation do not. One day, try eating something you think you do not like, and you may find it is not as bad as you assumed. If you don't try it, how will you get the nutrients present in that food? The body requires all essential nutrients for good health. If your body lacks certain nutrients it will affect your fitness. This means you should include foods of all tastes, even those with a bitter taste. Similarly, you should also learn to deal with bitter people.

Under the name of a festival, all types of vegetable are mixed together and presented in one dish to remind us how we must all live in harmony with one another in our relationships. As a result, we can receive a taste of every form of love, and liberate ourselves from the negativity of suspicion, deceit, attachment, and ego in our relations. In the next section, we shall learn how to remove this negativity.

Section II

HOW TO REMOVE NEGATIVITY FROM RELATIONSHIPS

4

*To live free is to live happily
by making others happy.*

What There Must Be in Relationships

Six steps in the ladder of relationships

Now, let us find out what every relationship needs to have. Relationships must be free from attachment and obsession. They must have a high level of consciousness and understanding to awaken the power of discrimination. This will help us know what is wrong and what is right in our relationships.

It has often been observed in our society that when someone's near and dear one dies, they remain sad for a very long time because of attachment. If they actually loved and were not merely attached to that person, and if they had the knowledge of life after death, then they would not feel sad. This means that attachment and ignorance are at the root of all such sorrow.

When we are dependent on people around us, we gradually begin to become their slaves. When we require someone's assistance for everything, we become lazy and avoid work. Others take advantage of this situation. They start using us like pawns for their needs. Do not become dependent on others; shed your attachment to all your supports. This does not mean you should never take help from others, but you must try to become independent. When the need arises, offer help to others and take help from others. But if you wish to lead a free life, if you want to be happy by making others happy, if you want to keep happiness close to your heart and sorrow at bay, then you will have to get rid of dependency on others.

Every relationship is a mirror for us. In some relations we witness the anger withheld within us, in others we witness our inner greed. Some relationships bring to light the hatred within, others reveal our attachments. Some relations arouse envy, while some hurt our ego. Some relationships may bring forth the fear hidden inside us, while some others reveal a loathing and malice buried deep within. We should not feel depressed on noticing these hidden aspects; instead we should realize the nature of our body–mind with understanding. The light of this understanding will wipe away the darkness within and you will be illuminated with the light of truth. In order to acquire this understanding, as well as to witness your nature, contemplate every relationship.

How do relationships form at each juncture of your life? What do you consider your relatives to be through your interactions with them? Understand this with the help of the ladder of relationships given below.

First step: When a child is small, his relationship with everything is: *'I and object – I and object,'* that is, he considers everything as lifeless. He throws one object on the other. Whether a glass breaks or a heart, it makes no difference to him. Breaking and throwing things is normal for him due to ignorance.

Second step: When the child grows up a bit, then his relationship with everything is: *'I and object – I and you.'* This means that he considers his parents and siblings as lifeless objects, while he regards objects as living entities. He begins to love his objects (pen, watch, computer, bike, toys, etc.) and stubbornly uses people as objects. He is completely inconsiderate towards their feelings.

Third step: When the child grows up some more and develops some maturity, his relationship with everything becomes: *'I and you – I and object.'* This means that he starts giving more importance to people than objects. He begins to understand their feelings. He feels love for them. Now he has learnt to treat humans as humans and objects as objects. At this stage, his behavior becomes oriented in the right direction.

Fourth step: When he develops further maturity on growing up, then his relationship with everything is: *'I and you – I and you,'* which means that not only does he respect people but he also gives respect to objects. Objects also contain the vibrations that we humans do – with this understanding, he stops throwing things around and starts keeping them in an organized manner. He stops banging the door and instead closes it gently. Supreme love begins to awaken within him towards everything.

Fifth step: After acquiring wisdom, when he becomes quite mature, his relationship with everything is: *'Object and object – object and object,'* that is, he understands that previously he had considered his body to be 'I' and the body in front of him as 'you'. In reality, 'I' and 'you' were not bodies, but he had interacted with them considering them to be bodies. In effect, this meant that objects had been interacting with objects. Now he learns to become a detached witness and observes the interactions between relationships. Upon reaching this state, he begins to understand the ultimate step, the last rung of this ladder.

Sixth step: When he becomes fully mature on attaining complete wisdom, his relationship with everything becomes: *'You and you – you and you,'* that is, he witnesses the Truth or Universal Self in everything. Now he knows that love alone is operating through every body and we are interacting with love alone. In this state, attachment of any sort is completely destroyed.

By learning about the six steps of this ladder, we have come to know the height of relationships that we can attain. In the next chapter, let us learn how we can always live with understanding and break attachment in our relationships.

5

*Once ignorance perishes, attachment vanishes
and a new light enters relationships.*

WHAT THERE MUST NOT BE IN RELATIONSHIPS

How attachment can be eliminated

Attachment may develop in relationships because of ignorance. This is the biggest problem. In order to get rid of attachment, ask yourself: "What can this attachment give me? What benefits will it deliver throughout my life? Is attachment or detachment most beneficial in relationships?" If you contemplate this topic in depth, there will be no attachment in your relationships, only true love.

Due to attachment, family members feel that their son, daughter, sister, or brother must be a top-of-class student and then become a great success in this world. People believe that their own children, family, and relatives are theirs; others are not theirs, others are all strangers. These beliefs are held by those who are unaware of the purpose of being born on Earth. For those who know the truth, relationships are not limited to a single family. They view everyone from a higher perspective. For them, the entire world is one family.

What is the cause of clashes in relationships? Clashes occur because people forget what should not be present in relationships. The *Mahabharata* is a great Indian epic, a religious book that describes a historic war. By studying the characters in the Mahabharata who were the cause of the war, we can understand what should not be present in relationships. We can learn from every character in the

Mahabharata about what you should and should not do to improve relationships.

When we consider Duryodhana (one of the Mahabharata's negative characters) we are reminded that ego should be absent in relationships. Ego leads to turmoil, and where it is present, disputes are bound to occur.

When considering Shakuni, we realize relationships must also be free from deceit and suspicion. Once there is lack of trust in a relationship, all conversation and communication falls into doubt. We question why this person is talking to that person. We feel we are being deliberately excluded. We experience mistrust, jealousy, and frustration. Everything in the relationship is suspected of deceit.

When we start doubting and deceiving, our relationships begin to break down. Suspicions prevailing between family members, neighbors, or colleagues lead to cessation of communication, with each suspecting the other from within. But unless one discusses the reasons for suspicion, how can a relationship be repaired? If the rift is not mended, it develops into an impenetrable wall, which rigidly separates people from each other.

Analyzing the character of Dhritarashtra, we realize his fault was wanting his son to become what he himself could not be. It is typical that a person unable to become a doctor, for example, wishes his son to become the doctor instead. The father's overwhelming desire is that his son should achieve what he could not. He forces his son into the medical profession, despite the son's aspiration from childhood to work with wood and become a carpenter. Now, how would his son perform with something as intricate as surgery? The father's obstinacy not only harms the child, it also risks harm to others.

The character of Dhritarashtra teaches us how personal aspirations operate. What he could not become himself, he forced on his children, believing his children to be his property. He was responsible to a large extent for his son Duryodhana being the obsessed man he was, because he wanted his son to become king. He added fuel to a fire that was already burning within Duryodhana. Duryodhana wanted the throne and Dhritarashtra endlessly supported him. Duryodhana's aspirations grew to such heights that it caused a colossal war, in which his entire family perished. Duryodhana was ambitious and egoistic, and was accompanied by the deceitful Shakuni. It is not surprising that such a lethal combination resulted in the destruction of a great family.

Duryodhana's mother, Gandhari, permanently blindfolded herself despite being able to see. Her blind husband, Dhritarashtra, was already stumbling and suffering, but rather than helping him she covered her eyes as well. This is indicative of ignorance and blind attachment. It made her unable to take the right stand in the quarrelsome relationships within her family. What follies are committed in ignorance! Everyone becomes dependent on another. The future of such a family is inevitably dark.

When people forget the purpose of coming to Earth, they become dependent and develop deep attachments. When someone feels, "Everyone should give me attention," they are unable to do anything when that attention isn't received. People invariably become dependent in attachment; in this case, to other people and the attention they give. They become pawns at the mercy of materialistic lures. Even if they can see that their situation is wrong, they are unable to say that it is unjust to steal others' rights, or to express that there is enough love, happiness, food, and work for everyone.

The character of Karna in the Mahabharata is a symbol of dependence and helplessness. Due to his overbearing sense of debt to his benefactor Duryodhana, he stood by Duryodhana even though he was aware that he was supporting the wrong side. Relationships must be devoid of such debilitating factors. Do not support wrong people or wrong causes out of dependence or false obligation. Sacrifice out of love, not out of helplessness.

When the coarse Dushyasana, brother of Duryodhana, enters these legendary relationships, there can only be anarchy and violence. Dushyasana treated his cousins' wife Draupadi in the most disrespectful manner because he regarded her as merely an object, a slave who could be mistreated and commanded at will. Many people treat their family members the same way; if not so violently, then in a similar thoughtless and indifferent manner. They do not see a difference between their mother or spouse and the television set or sofa. They will order about their wife, their children, or their siblings as if pressing the remote control and expecting obedience. When there is such meanness in the family, it will undoubtedly lead to tension, despair, sorrow, and conflict.

Learning of the characters of the Mahabharata, you will be convinced that if helpless, suspicious, greedy, deceitful, obsessed, and egoistic people are present in a family, then war will be inevitable. A family should be free from suspicion, ego, deceit, violence, attachment, and individualistic aspirations. We have to free ourselves from these vices to save our family tree from being destroyed, and to attain peace, joy, love, and contentment in the family.

6

Whoever attains harmony in feelings, thoughts, words, and actions, decides there is no need to do anything secretively.

How to Save Your Family Tree From Being Cut Down
The saw of ego and the axe of deceit

A family is like a tree. The character of society takes shape under its shade. Consumed by greed, people start cutting down this tree. They destroy the tree of love with the saw of ego and the axe of deceit. We must protect our family tree from these deadly weapons.

The main reason why relationships become strained in a family is the desire of some family members to take command. Overcome by this desire, they start to employ deceit. To make their lies appear to be true, more lies enter the family space. Only by achieving freedom from all such lies can a family lead a joyful life.

No family member should desire to have sole control over the family. By following such a path, one's level of consciousness falls and one gets trapped in unnecessary matters. The desire to show off our ego and increase our sense of importance only moves us away from our ultimate goal on Earth. In such a state, we perform our activities with only our image in mind. We feel that if we said 'no' to something in the past, how can we say 'yes' to the same thing now? For a person seeking control, saying 'yes' after saying 'no', or vice versa, becomes extremely hard. It's difficult to admit that our earlier thinking was wrong or we made a mistake because we did not have complete information. Rather than admit our mistake, we continue baseless argument and debate to prove we are right and in control. This very effort fills relationships with darkness.

Every member of the family should understand that when information for making decisions is lacking, then other family members will openly be told. By divulging the truth, the entire family will begin to trust and support each other. The fact is people support those who are deceit-free. People who are trustworthy and can speak without deceit are chosen for great work because this is what great work requires.

It won't harm you if you openly admit your mistakes in front of your family. Changing your 'no' to a 'yes' or your 'yes' to a 'no' makes no big difference. Your image is not degraded; rather, people will like you for your honest attitude. But the fact is that we always want to appear 'different' from others, which is why we stubbornly stick to our point.

Only after getting rid of ego can you realize that all members of a family are like fingers of the same hand. Initially, people can accept this idea at an intellectual level, only later, when the new light of wisdom dawns upon them, do they understand it from experience. Thereafter, they are able to accept every finger as it is, whether big or small, fat or thin. Ego vanishes in the feeling of acceptance.

A family does not progress much when only one person is contributing to it. If all members work together, it can progress faster. In a family, some members may be open, while others may have resistance towards certain issues. By working together, even those who feel themselves weak individually will start opening up. When some can put their egos aside, others will be able to grow and blossom.

Family members may sometimes hide activities from each other in order to achieve personal aspirations. At such times, they will say they are doing one thing when in fact they are doing another. Such behavior gives rise to various problems in the family.

As members of the family become increasingly deceit-free, they stop doing things secretively. The real person inside is then the same as their external expression of themselves. When they are able to speak honestly, they stop being afraid that someone will think ill of them, mock them, or obstruct their work.

To help you gain a new perspective on this subject, here are some questions: Can you say in how many relationships will you be able to become completely honest before leaving this world? What have you done to enable people to talk with you honestly? What do you do for people to enable them to trust you? Are people able to give you unconditional love? Are they able to open up their hearts to you? To get an honest answer to all these questions, you must first of all know yourself. Understand that there are several aspects to the making or breaking of any relationship, but usually we are only able to see a few. Only by knowing yourself can you bring about a change in your outlook. When everyone starts speaking to you honestly, then you will be able to scale the heights of relationships.

With a full understanding of the complete aim of life, you would want to know all the secrets of the world. But you remain in the darkness of ignorance because people do not speak honestly to you. Therefore, all your assumptions about them, in fact, are wrong. When people speak to you honestly, it is then that you can understand that they are inherently good, and only under certain circumstances do they behave badly. If their fears were removed, they would never behave badly at all.

We may think that a particular person is bad because their nature is not good. But such wrong assumptions are dissolved merely by listening and speaking sincerely. When they speak to you openly, even for a short while, you learn about their real troubles, fears, aspirations, beliefs, inner thoughts, and so on. Only by listening to their genuine words can you gauge the underlying greed, fear, or other emotions that lie behind their conversation. When you learn the truth and realize their feelings, you will feel the need for compassion, love, and sympathy; not for dislike or hatred of such a person. You remain in the dark only because people do not speak honestly to you. Because of this, we can spend our entire lives in the dark and also die in the dark, without understanding the true nature of people. When you recognize this reality of life, you will reach the heights of relationships.

The person in the family who becomes one – in feelings, thoughts, actions, and words – can declare: "I wish to be an open book and live my life free of deceit. I do not wish to do anything secretively. Kindly help me to attain this goal." Such people display openness in all relationships and are loved by all.

The earlier you become deceit-free in relationships, and experience oneness, the sooner you can say, "Now, I do not need to remember what I said earlier to whom or what I should say now." In this way, you will be saved from the vicious circle of lies, because to cover one lie you need a thousand more. This is how the axe of deceit cuts down your family tree. So keep the saw of ego and the axe of deceit away. To save your family from disintegration and to keep the branches, leaves, and flowers of your family tree flourishing harmoniously, keep watering the tree with your love.

7

*Love can be received only by giving;
not by demanding.*

How to Fill The Love Bank Of Your Family
Understand the dictionary of your family members

The Oxford dictionary defines 'love' in various ways such as: 'deep affection or fondness,' 'to delight in,' or 'to like very much'. However, each one of us is actually moving around with our own personal dictionary in our minds.

Our dictionary comprises words that are defined by our past experiences, judgments, and biases. In other words, our dictionary is a repository of preconceived notions and beliefs that are shaped by our past. Therefore, the mental dictionary of each one of us is different. To better understand others, we need to read their dictionaries. When we start reading and understanding others' mental dictionaries, we will find they no longer seem to be 'others'. We will be able to identify what drives their thoughts, words, and actions, and feel compassion and empathy. This will help us build a common communication platform. We can at least do this with the members of our family. The meaning of words as you understand them may not necessarily be the same as the interpretations made by your brother, sister, parents, partner, or in-laws.

All members of a family wish well for each other, so why do quarrels take place? Everyone wants harmony in the family, so why do ill feelings arise between family members? The reason is that nobody has paused for a while to consider the other person's dictionary. Everyone is concerned only about their own dictionary. Some people do not even review their own dictionary. Those who always proceed from their own mental dictionary, feel and act as if their interpretation of 'love' (or any other word for that matter) is the universal truth. However, your definition of love may be interpreted as a criticism or a punishment by others. You ought to check with the other person whether their interpretation matches yours. It is only then you may realize that, apart from some commonalities, their dictionary largely varies from your own.

The more you get to know about each other's dictionary, the more a common platform of understanding can begin to be established between you. It needs frequent focused discussions to make this platform concrete.

Love Bank

We need to contemplate the relationships in our life in which we are able to experience love and happiness. Who are these important family members who perhaps enable us to go to work without worry knowing someone is taking care of everything at home, or spend their day at work to enable us to rest at home free from worries?

After identifying them, we have to contemplate what we are doing for these relations. Do we do anything special for them? In most cases, we may realize that we do not do anything for them. We take them for granted. We think: "This is their duty; they are doing what I expect them to." Upon reflection, we may also realize that there are only a few such relations in our life; perhaps there are one, two, three, or at the most four such people who really matter. What do we do for them? We may work the whole day to earn money to feed the family, but when it is time to actually eat, we hardly devote five minutes to those around us. We earn and build our finances to have a secure family life, but are we able to express our love to our family members?

There is a love bank inside each person, the balance of which fluctuates every day. The key is to ensure that the love bank never gets empty. The balance that is available in this bank determines the joy, peace, and love in the family.

The currency that each person's love bank accepts varies depending on their definition of love. You need to understand the dictionary of the other person in order to know which currency you should deposit in their love bank.

The different currencies that fill the love banks of people are discussed below.

1. Gifts

Some people feel they are loved only if they receive gifts. If such people's definition of love is unknown to their family they will remain unhappy, even though the family may cater to them in all other ways. It could be that you actually give this person the most expensive of gifts, yet still find they remain dissatisfied. You need to understand the type of things they like in order to know what items to give. It is not essential that your gift should be expensive. Even a simple flower or a greeting card can work wonders with such a person.

The important point is that they should feel they have been considered and are loved as a result of your gift. With the right gifts, your balance in their love bank will rise and they will be prepared to reciprocate your gestures of love. Even if they do not reciprocate, you should not feel concerned. Your gifts should be selfless gestures for your own happiness; expressions of unconditional love. Do not lose this impersonal perspective by considering what you will receive in return. Your smallest expressions of consideration can fill another's life with love and bliss.

2. Time

For some people, gifts do not matter. Their definition of love is based on the amount of time that is spent with them. You may feel confused about why this person is unhappy even when you do so much for them. But this person feels they are loved only when someone spends 'exclusive' time with them. You may feel you show your love by ensuring the family's needs are met. But to fulfil this person's definition of love, you need to spend time at their side. Once their love bank is full, they will reciprocate your love. Bear in mind, however, that the time you spend with them should be exclusively for them and not just small talk while watching television.

3. Appreciation in words

Some people do not feel happy even when you give them ample gifts or spend many hours in their company. It is only when you appreciate them wholeheartedly that they feel genuinely happy. Acknowledging their achievements on accomplishing even a small task, or providing feedback to show your interest in work they have done, is the way to unlock their happiness. They will then regard you as the most generous person in the world. They will feel that you admire their efforts and understand what they are doing. You need to closely observe what each member of your family is engaged in. Once they receive your appreciation, they will continue even more enthusiastically with their activities. Appreciation will fill their love bank and they will reciprocate with love. This approach will also help to maintain harmony and positivity in the family.

4. Service

Some people do not feel happy with any of the things mentioned above. Their love bank is filled only when you serve them in some way. For example, if parents are able to help their children in preparing for their day at school – by packing their school bag, preparing their snacks, readying them with their school uniform – then the children feel loved by their parents.

Even a wife may feel that her husband loves her only if he helps her with household activities. When he helpfully joins her in this work, she then reciprocates his love by meeting his wishes. But until he shows this understanding, she feels he does not love her, despite his buying gifts or taking her for expensive meals. She feels he is doing these things to satisfy his own need rather than to please her. As soon as he starts doing minor household activities, like helping with cleaning or ironing his own clothes, it makes her feel that her husband loves her. The day he reads and understands her dictionary, he is amazed to find that even small services bring her immense happiness.

Some husbands may come from a parental background where it was believed that men shouldn't be involved in household work. This could make it difficult for the couple to be happy. The husband should discover and fulfill the needs of his wife and not follow the practice of his parents. This is because his parents may have had their own definition of love.

5. Touch

People who belong to this last category feel they are loved only when they receive someone's touch. Children who feel this way wish for their parents to hug them before leaving the house. Once they receive your touch, they feel a sense of love. Their love bank is filled. Many children who grow up in orphanages are devoid of a loving touch throughout childhood. The result is that they always feel a void; by being neglected their love bank remains empty.

Aged parents often feel the need for their grown up children to touch them. But their children think that in childhood they hugged their parents so much, it is unnecessary now. When parents cannot communicate their deep longing and children do not understand them, life ends in an unfulfilled way. But now that you know this, you must respond and see the results.

Every member of your family has a different dictionary. You need to get to know their dictionaries through focused meetings in order to understand each other. Some will immediately read out their dictionaries to you, while others will not feel like revealing theirs at all. Those who are ready to communicate will take the initiative. Others may fear being ridiculed, or feel ashamed, and will need careful and gentle encouragement.

When you practice identifying people's dictionaries and filling their love banks accordingly, you will get miraculous results. When you see such wonderful results, you surely will be encouraged to continue. However, you should continue this valuable practice regardless of whether or not you experience results.

Remember too, even if someone's love bank is filled today, tensions of any kind can rapidly reduce it or even leave it empty in just a few days. Then your appreciative words, your little gestures of help, your small gifts, a kind touch, or a few minutes of exclusive time will be needed to refill the bank.

Just imagine, if interpreting the meaning of just one word – love – in another's dictionary can work such wonders, how marvelous your relations could be if you learnt the whole of your family members' dictionaries completely!

In the next chapter, let us see what should be avoided in relationships to keep love alive.

8

*True love is free from insecurity, suspicion, and doubt.
True love does not ask evidence of love.*

How to Keep Love Alive in Relationships
Proof of love and the end of love

Relationships full of love indicate abundant happiness. Relationships devoid of love just make a lot of noise like empty vessels. To fill our relationships to the brim with love, we must understand the chemistry of love. The element called love contracts on being exposed to the air of suspicion and expands when exposed to the fragrance of trust. With the help of this catalyst called trust, let us permeate the world of relations with the element of love.

Many people feel the lack of love in their relations. They wonder why they do not feel the same degree of love towards each and every person. Why do they express their love differently in different relationships? Why is there more love in blood relations and less in distant relations?

Our expression of love is different with different people because our level of consciousness varies in relation to different people. Therefore, we feel more love in some relationships and do not feel any love in others. However, when we attain the highest wisdom, our level of consciousness rises to such an extent that we feel love for everyone. We feel oneness with the whole of creation.

Negative emotions reappear unknowingly when our level of consciousness drops. Under the influence of negative emotions, our relationships attract such attitudes as: "This person does what I tell him, so I like him… that person never does anything for me, so I don't like him… the other person sometimes helps me and sometimes doesn't, so I find him okay… but this person is my brother, so I like him, and I'm happy my duty is to look after his well-being…"

In some cases, you love someone more because you spend more time with them. The love you experience in that case may be from a sense of duty or because your relationship is close. You are also likely to love anyone who supports you or boosts your ego. However, when your level of consciousness rises higher, you realize that every person, in fact, is in love with their own shopping list. Everyone has a shopping list that they carry around with them all the time. It lists such wants as: love or attention, help, money, good food, jewelry, entertainment, and so on. Such a shopping list exists inside each one of us. We meet people every day while carrying this shopping list in our head. Then, we think, "This person can fulfil a wish of mine, and that person can fulfil another one of my wishes." If someone gives us what we want, we feel that person loves us. If someone cannot fulfil any of our wishes, we assume they do not love us. In this way, we like those who help us get what we want, and we do not like those who do not. Thus, we lead our lives on the basis of a shopping list, which results in struggle, unhappiness, stress, and misery in relationships.

Do you love people or your stories about them?

In addition to the shopping list aspect, do you wonder whether you really love people or just your opinions about them? Are they really dear to you? Or is it your stories about them that are dear to you? The reality is that if the yarn you have spun about people is to your liking, then you feel you love those people. If you have spun a negative yarn, then you do not feel positive about them. If you are told something bad about someone, then your story (opinion) about that person changes and you develop negative feelings about them. In this case, is the person actually bad, or is it just your opinion about them that is bad?

The key point to understand is that there is nothing happening 'out there' in the external world. The game of like and dislike is being played within the mind. The misery that we go through in relationships is owing to our thoughts and the stories that we cook up in our mind. Similarly, the fleeting joys that we experience are also due to the labels that we attach to the people and events in our life. We hardly ever pause to ponder upon this intricate truth.

Prove your love

We have the habit of demanding that others prove their love for us. We never doubt our own love but always doubt whether the other person loves us or not. This person has to prove their love by giving something to us. We demand this because we have the tendency to suspect everything; we remain surrounded by doubts and make wrong assumptions time and again.

As individuals, we always feel the need to check whether the other person loves us today as much as they did yesterday. Has their love diminished or disappeared? The underlying fear is of what might happen to us if their love is gone. How will our wishes be fulfilled? It is due to this insecurity that we want the other person to prove their love.

A miser opens his treasury, counts his money, and only then is he able to get down to work. He needs to count his money every single day. He wants daily proof that he still has all his money because he is scared of losing it. Similarly, if we do not trust the other person, and are ignorant of true love, we will constantly demand proof of love. But by demanding proof again and again, we actually kill their love. The constant checking for love troubles the other person, who feels, "Why do I have to prove my love every day?" For example, if one day a husband does not bring flowers for his wife, she thinks his love for her has reduced. She does not consider that there could be a thousand other reasons for not bringing flowers.

People also kill their own happiness in this way by always suspecting their happiness. The slightest boredom makes us feel, "I don't feel as joyful as before. I do not feel as good today as I did yesterday." After such thoughts, we feel depressed. We need to be reminded that love and joy are always available within us; it is only their expression that is more obvious at some times and less so at other times.

We also demand people prove their love for us in order to impose our own ways of expressing love. We think, "They should use the same words that I use when I love someone." We always desire such proofs. Yet proof is needed only when something is not steady and true. This is why proof is needed to overcome doubt in a court of law; otherwise there would be no need for evidence. Thus, it is better that you maintain this understanding in every situation and not try to bind others by demanding evidence of love from them. In this way, their love for you will be sustained. Otherwise what little love is left will be lost due to your imposing behavior.

It has often been noted that a mother loves her son unconditionally, but when he gets married she tries to protect him from her daughter-in-law. The mother feels insecure and suspects her son may stop paying attention to her. Initially, the son finds his mother's behavior strange. All his life, he loved his mother dearly because she spoke with him openly and directly. She had no hidden agenda and always behaved as her natural self. Now, with the arrival of a daughter-in-law, his mother has begun speaking in an indirect manner. The son feels something is amiss because his mother never behaved this way before. After several years of this troubling behavior, the unquestioned love between mother and son ceases to exist and both demand proofs of love from each other. True love has eroded, as demands for evidence of love has resulted in the destruction of love. In order to maintain love, do not seek proof of love.

Choose love

Generally, people feel they can express love only when they experience the right feeling. They think, "I never feel like speaking nicely to this person, so I won't unless I feel like it." However, does a student say, 'I won't study until I feel like it'? Those who fall into this trap fail their examinations. But sincere students decide, "I don't feel like studying, but I do have a choice. I want to achieve my goals, so I will study even when I don't feel like it." Similarly, even if we do not feel love, we can choose love. We need to realize that we are making choices every moment of our life. Those who can understand this, change their approach. They choose love in all circumstances. If we keep waiting for the feeling to arise, we will never be able to love all through our life. Hence, make a higher choice. Choose love. And keep loving relationships away from suspicions and assumptions.

9

Words are empty vessels;
it is unfortunate if you remain entangled in them.

HOW TO ESCAPE FROM THE SWORD OF WORDS IN RELATIONSHIPS

The curse of suspicion and assumption

There was a big family. It consisted of all manner of relatives – brothers, sisters, mothers, fathers, grandmothers, grandfathers, and so on. Everyone lived together in unconditional love and true happiness. One day, a fake, or perhaps just a deceitful, relative visited the family. He began to talk loudly in an engaging, enthusiastic, and knowing manner. With his encouraging words and subtle ways, the whole family was soon aroused into a sense of gaiety, entertainment, and false happiness. Several family members thought they truly admired his ways with his rousing conversation and big laughter. His words gave them false pleasure.

Some people are more than pleased to hear words that create fake happiness. Wherever such people meet, they start bad-mouthing and back-biting others, or use witty words and racy stories to make people laugh, and an environment of false happiness is created.

Almost every classroom in every school has one or more children who pass comments while the teacher is conducting the class. When they comment, the other children laugh and enjoy the disruption. When the naughty child is absent from school, the other children feel it was a boring day. Students heavily burdened with studies and classes can derive some pleasure from the distracting words of a mischievous pupil. But, unfortunately, this mischievous pupil is hardly able to learn anything. He sits in class thinking, "What should I say now? Which joke should I crack that will tickle others?" He thinks this way during each and every lecture. Because of this, he learns nothing, but remains focused on creating fake cheerfulness with his funny words. He is unaware that his habit is destroying his future.

Similarly, when the false relative enters the house, the family starts thinking about their words. Earlier, they would talk among themselves but would pay less attention to the words themselves and more attention to the underlying meaning. They knew that, for them, the importance of words lay only in understanding whatever the words were intended to express. Words are empty vessels; it is unfortunate if you remain entangled in them.

Coming back to the story, on one occasion the elderly grandmother wanted a bowl that rested high on a shelf. When one of her grandsons tried to fetch it, she told him, "Dear! You are short and your brother is tall, so he will be able to get the bowl." At that moment, the deceitful relative told the shorter man, "Hear that? She is calling you short and your brother tall. She shouldn't speak like that. She should say he is taller and you are less tall." With this, the shorter man started feeling depressed thinking himself considered inferior in comparison to others.

When comparisons and misunderstandings begin in the mind, they lead to hatred in relationships. When the human mind starts comparing, it is bound to make assumptions. When the mind foregoes the meaning and instead gets involved in words, it is then that assumptions start being made. This results in comparisons between relations and conflicts within the family.

Assumption is a seed that requires no watering. From assumption arises suspicion, which needs no watering either. As is the seed, so is the fruit; assumption and suspicion continue to grow by themselves. When these seeds germinate in people's minds, people look at one another with assumptions and suspicion. Such assumptions as "This person definitely thinks badly of me" cause rifts in relationships.

Finally in the story, a well-wisher makes an entry. He makes the family members return to their happy natural state and reveals to them the truth of their experience. He explains to them how they had lost their true happiness by getting stuck in deceitful words, how they had been caught up in false happiness, and how their attention was diverted from true love and joy. Suspicion and assumptions are the weapons that false relatives use.

By listening to the well-wisher and understanding the meaning of his words, the trick being played by the fake relative comes to light. No one in the family is prepared now to believe what the trickster says. The trickster therefore leaves in search of another family. Has he ended up at your place, by any chance?

10

Accepting life as it is will bring out the better person inside you and lead you toward the best life.

How Can An Understanding Family Become A Happy Family

Keep track of the stress levels in your family

Relationships are held together by a delicate thread. This thread can easily be broken by a small tug of carelessness. When this thread is anointed with awareness, it becomes as strong as the string that pulls a kite. If any member of the family is passing through a phase of mental stress, once the rest of the family is aware of this they can help them to overcome the problem.

In order to maintain peaceful relations, it is important to be aware of any stress in the family. This is easily possible with a 'stress level chart'.

By putting up a daily 'stress level description chart' on the family notice-board, the husband, wife, brothers, sisters, grandparents, and everyone can communicate freely with each other. They can have positive dialogues between themselves by establishing this common platform for communication. Through the stress level chart, everyone will know about each other's mental state, and thereby be able to take appropriate steps to lower each other's tensions.

It is essential to know the mental states of all family members. If we are aware of the mental states and the reasons for any distress, the family together can help to overcome such stress. If we cannot eliminate an individual's stress, then at least we can avoid enhancing it. Through the stress level chart, we can learn of the problems and expectations of each family member.

Perhaps a member of the family needs our help or our love, or they simply want to share the experiences of the day. How would we know? Perhaps, they require advice from us, or want to tell us that they are hurt by our behavior. The stress chart can lower any tensions that have developed within the family.

As soon as a member of the family returns home from work, market, school, or college, they will first take a look at the notice-board. On the notice-board, the names of the family members will be displayed, and next to the names will be pinned a piece of paper. The paper could be red, green, yellow, or a piece of newspaper. Based on the kind of paper beside each name, the mental state of each can be gauged.

Stress Level Chart

Happy Home   **Date:**

No.	Name	Paper	Mental State
1	W	Red	Angry, serious: Do not disturb
2	X	Yellow	Intermediate between red and green: Neutral state
3	Y	Green	Happy and receptive
4	Z	Newspaper	Very troubled and full of thoughts
5	You	?	?

Thus, when members of the family enter the house and look at the papers on the chart, they will know how they should behave towards their family members and what kind of response is needed.

They will understand how serious is the stress level of any individual family member, and the degree of overall stress at home.

If we see a red paper against someone's name (say W) on the notice-board, we understand that W's state is serious. They are angry, and should not be disturbed under any condition.

If we see a yellow paper next to X's name, it signifies that everything is normal and okay. This is an intermediate state of mind between red and green.

If there is a green paper next to Y's name, it means Y is happy and receptive. Y is ready to welcome you and listen to you if you have something to share with him or her. Together you can plan to lower the stress levels of the rest of the family.

If there is a newspaper next to Z's name, it indicates that person is troubled and lost in a storm of thoughts. They need silence and solitude. So, leave them alone for a while.

Once you have added your own stress level to the chart, everyone will be able to help each other appropriately, in good time, and without unnecessarily aggravating anyone's distress.

When all stress signals are either yellow or green, happiness can spread throughout the family. It is possible for all to open up completely and express themselves joyfully. That day is the family's Diwali, Eid, or Christmas. If everyone is in high spirits in the family, then isn't it a festive occasion? Why wait for a festival to celebrate joy? Merely displaying stress levels on a notice-board can work wonders for a family.

For your own stress level chart, you do not need to follow exactly the example above. You can discuss options together and use your imagination to come up with alternative techniques, symbols, pictures or words. Whatever your own family stress chart looks like, you will find it a very effective tool for controlling tensions in relationships.

11

When a person repents in the right manner,
they become renewed and liberated from guilt.

TO IMPROVE RELATIONSHIPS, FIRST IMPROVE YOURSELF

How to say 'sorry'

To improve relationships, do not blame others but improve yourself. When we make a mistake with others, we should admit it and apologize. But is repentance complete on just saying 'sorry'? When, and how, should we say sorry in relationships?

Imagine a family where people can easily ask for forgiveness from each other in the right manner. How much love and joy there would be in that family! However, many people find it difficult to even say sorry. Their ego is challenged by the act of apologizing. We need to overcome the power of the ego and serve relationships instead. We can achieve freedom from guilt by asking for forgiveness in the right way.

The great saints of every religion have shown various ways to attain liberation from guilt and begin a new life. Jesus was one such liberator. He blessed and liberated from guilt those who were sinners and even prostitutes. People did not approve of his behavior. Therefore, to explain his actions and inspire others to do the same, Jesus told a story.

There was a man who had two sons. The younger son had fallen prey to many vices, which left him bankrupt. He filed a lawsuit against his father to get his share of the family's property. The attitude of the younger son enraged the elder son, but the father remained calm. He said, "His money and his share in the property must be given to him." The younger son took his share and left the village.

After many years, with all his wealth squandered, he returned to the village. When his father learnt of his arrival, he went to receive him. He learnt that his younger son had returned to repent for his bad behavior. The father received his son with joy and threw a grand party to celebrate his homecoming.

When the elder son, who was working hard in the fields, learnt that his younger brother had returned after losing all his money, and his father was to hold a feast for his reception, he felt very dejected. He thought, "My father has never organized any feast for me, although I am good and obedient. He shouldn't be doing this for my brother who is evil and egoistic."

After returning from the fields, the elder son questioned his father, "Why are you doing this? My brother has behaved so badly, yet you are hosting a feast to celebrate his return. I have never behaved badly like him, but you have never done any such thing for me." The father replied, "On the contrary, you should be happy that your brother who was dead has come back alive; who was lost in material illusions has now come back to his senses." On hearing this, the elder son fell silent. What could he say? The father explained, "You were always before my eyes, hence you feel I have not done anything for you, but this is not true. Which child does the father worry about more? The one who is good and near, or the one who is lost and a sinner?" The elder son understood what his father meant, and his doubts were erased.

Those who were listening to Jesus also received an answer to their doubts. Sinners also have a right to repentance. Every individual must get a chance to begin a new life. Jesus said, "The Lord forgives with love all those sinners who seek repentance." Thus, God forgives those who accept their wrongdoings and those who repent. But to repent is not merely to say, "O Dear God, forgive my sins." Repentance is to tell God honestly, "I am guilty of committing these particular sins with these particular intentions. I hurt these people, and for this I ask Your forgiveness." Narrating your sins in detail before God, and praying for forgiveness, is true repentance.

People often pray superficially "O God, please forgive our sins" but thereafter do not change their conduct. They say, "God knows everything that we do, so why do we need to describe our sins in detail to Him?" Understand that when you confess your sins with deep feeling, when you describe them in detail, you will feel both the responsibility and the release from those sins.

It is not enough to just say sorry. Merely saying sorry is not true repentance and does not yield any result. One must confess to those who have suffered from your behavior and say, "I did this. I hurt you. I am ashamed of it. Please forgive me." If you are able to say all of this, then you become responsible; and those who have suffered will understand your repentance. You must understand the feelings of the other person, and ask for forgiveness from the depth of your heart.

It may be that while saying sorry to someone, they tell you, "There is no need to repent. I wasn't hurt by your behavior. Please don't worry." In spite of this, you should say, "I have committed a mistake. I won't repeat it in the future. Whether or not you were hurt, I am asking for forgiveness because this is God's wish. Please forgive me." This is the right way to repent.

When a person repents, they become renewed and begin a new, pure life. If your mind is full of love, faith, and thirst for liberation from guilt, then it is possible to attain freedom from this guilt. Write down all the mistakes that you have committed on a piece of paper. Then, in a safe place and with a pure mind and heart, light the paper and let it be consumed in fire, air, and dust. Now consider yourself free and able to begin a new life. A new life teaches you to seek forgiveness whenever you go wrong and to communicate this in the right manner with your family or those affected.

How to Communicate in Relationships in The Right Manner

12

*Obnoxious words and sarcasm
can have a deep impact on the victim of such abuse.*

Choose Words That Bring Warmth in Relations

Learn the magic of a soft and gentle voice

When we are learning a new language, we focus on the correct use and pronunciation of words. However, we rarely pay the same attention to the words that we use in our relationships. Truthful, but bitter, words do not generate good feelings. Likewise, pleasant words said with the wrong feeling can never yield good results. Therefore, in our relationships, it is critical to pay attention to our use of words and the way they are expressed.

To avoid tensions in relationships, we must first resolve that *we will never speak ill of others and never use bad words under any circumstances.* If tension develops in a relationship, never raise your voice but always speak softly. Whatever the circumstances, no matter what calamity may have befallen, do not hurl abusive words at others. In stressful situations, raising the voice and shouting offensive words only worsens the situation. Some people are quick to swear, even over small incidents, because it is a habit they have formed from childhood. They may not even notice or remember swearing because it is so habitual. But this harmful attitude should be avoided.

Remember that obnoxious words and sarcasm can have a deep impact on the victim of such abuse. The impact may last even a lifetime. If your harsh words hurt someone, then whatever help they might offer in a situation will be withdrawn. Such criticism escalates the tension in your relationship and makes it harder to receive cooperation in future. It is often said that hardships never come singly. We may be responsible for creating more problems for ourselves through our own bad habits and lack of control over our tongue.

When problems occur, we are easily tempted to express frustration and anger. But if we thoughtlessly give expression to such anger, it can quickly spread to all involved. We can find ourselves reacting irritably even to those who just want to help us. They will say: "I was only asking if I could offer assistance, but you reacted so badly that I won't offer to help you again." By speaking harshly to friends, colleagues, or relatives, you will lose their support. This will further aggravate your situation.

A vicious cycle of problems and stress continues when we fail to use our words with care. If you want to come out of this cycle, then you must first resolve: "I will never indulge in third-person talk." This means you will never speak ill of anyone who is not present. When speaking about someone who is not present you must resolve: "I will talk about them as if they are present. I will not criticize them or complain about them, and will only speak well of them."

With a firm resolve not to shout, swear, or employ abusive language about other people, either directly or indirectly, you will not make mistakes even in tense situations. To ensure continued good relations, you can also tell yourself: "I will not say anything about anyone that I cannot endorse in writing with my own signature." This will keep you constantly alert. You will always choose your words carefully and with awareness while speaking. Misunderstandings in relationships can thus be avoided.

13

*Always convey the right information
at the right time.*

STOP MISCOMMUNICATION IN RELATIONSHIPS
How to clear up misunderstandings

When you are trying to make a person understand, you will never be successful if that person is not willing, or able, to understand. Therefore, before trying, it is important to assess whether that person is ready to understand or not. We should not assume that another lacks understanding. Often, they simply are a victim of misunderstanding.

When people in a family converse to convey understanding of some matter, it is called communication. But due to lack of the 'art of communication' gaps in understanding can simply widen, which can cause rifts in relationships. So, come, let us get rid of misunderstandings in the family.

It is not possible to avoid communication. We communicate all the time, through our body language, our words, and our facial expressions. However, it is easy to convey wrong or incomplete information (miscommunication) to others, and this can lead to stress in relations. Misunderstandings can crop up, often unknowingly, between you and other people. If one member of the family is under stress while speaking, then that stress can be transmitted to the entire family. In this way, relations become tense, but this is often merely due to miscommunication.

In relationships, people often complain about each other, saying, "This is what she was doing... this is what he was saying..." When we listen to such complaints we feel uncomfortable. Later, when we meet the subject of those complaints, we are filled with uncharitable thoughts. We recall the negative things we have been told and they color our feelings. Previously, we always spoke to this person perfectly cordially. Now we feel disappointment and anger because we have accepted the negative talk of another. This is how misunderstandings are created within the family.

You must not indulge in such miscommunication, even without any ill-felt intentions. You may feel you are simply having a conversation, but in fact you may be conveying criticism, which you expect others to accept. Complaining, bad-mouthing, and back-biting can become a habit. You must break this habit. By breaking the habit of complaining as well as listening to complaints, relationships will not be spoilt and tensions will not grow.

If tensions increase in a relationship, those affected sometimes prefer to become silent. That is, they pass from miscommunication (misunderstanding) to no communication. But not communicating is also a form of communication. By not speaking to someone we are in fact conveying anger. Then the other person repeatedly asks, "Are you angry with me? Tell me what is wrong." Finally, from irritation, the silence ends, anger opens up and wrong things are said.

People can fall prey to misunderstandings in various situations, but the results can be devastating for families. You may have watched such situations in television soaps. To create drama, the script demands misunderstandings between the characters. If at all you want to watch such soaps, it could be as lessons teaching the type of misunderstandings you should avoid in real life.

Sometimes television and films present us with a clear picture of how misunderstandings arise and sensible ways to resolve them. In one such film, two colleagues have fallen out of communication due to misunderstandings between each other. Unable to face or speak to his colleague, one of them writes a letter to the other. The letter begins with good wishes, then lists all the good qualities of the other that have sustained their friendship. Only finally is the complaint that has kept them apart addressed, in gentle and reasonable terms. After delivering this letter to his colleague, their disagreements are amicably resolved.

Written communications can work in different and more subtle ways than direct speech. To enhance unity amongst the family, you may wish to experiment by writing letters and greeting cards. But you should contemplate before performing any experiment in order to know which aspects of your communications you need to improve. The reasons for misunderstandings between people are usually very small. Often, misunderstandings arise because we do not fully remember what we have been told or what we said. During our interactions, many a time the concerned person is unable to understand us, and neither are they able to tell us that they could not understand. Therefore misunderstandings occur.

When we are in conversation, we do not ask the listener to repeat our message to ensure it is correctly received, because we feel that they must be busy. One word or another can have different meanings for different people. If the listener is not familiar with our style of conversation, this can easily result in our being misunderstood.

If we receive wrong or incomplete information about a certain matter, it is all too easy for this wrong information to be passed on to others. On the other hand, we often do not feel the need to give certain information to others. But information that may seem minor to you, may mean a lot to someone else. Therefore, cultivate the habit of passing on information as soon as possible to anyone concerned. That would be a good use of telephone, email, and texting!

Sometimes we prefer not to convey information in order to avoid our own or others' discomfort. Such lack of action can result in much larger problems later on. So, no matter how unpleasant it may feel, even if you will be subject to rebuke, do pass on the right message at the right time. This will save you from a lot of potential trouble in the future.

Making wrong assumptions about people also causes misunderstandings. We may assume someone's reasons for doing something and duly pass our assumptions to others. But our assumptions may be completely wrong, so we should avoid spreading rumors and speak only when we know the truth.

Remember always to pay attention when someone speaks to you. If something else is going on in your mind, or you are distracted, there is a strong possibility you will misunderstand what is said.

How to clear up misunderstandings

To avoid misunderstandings, yet convey important information to the right people at the right time, you can use mutually agreed words and gestures that will indicate you are not angry.

If you wish to remain silent for a while, then simply indicate this with a hand gesture. The other person will then give you time and space, and allow you to be alone for a time.

To stop the illness of misunderstanding, erase the causes of this illness. Contemplate all the causes of misunderstandings in this chapter and devise an action plan for communicating with people henceforward. Subsequently, neither the causes, nor the misunderstandings themselves, will remain.

14

*Be aware of the nature of others
and respond to all with understanding.*

NEITHER THINK ALOUD NOR REMAIN SILENT
The root cause of problems in relations: 'Be like me'

Can two people named *Talkthink* and *Thinktalk* live happily under the same roof? As you read this, you may now be thinking, "What on earth does this mean?" or you might even express your confusion out loud if there is someone with you. To explain, *Talkthink* indicates a person whose habit is first to talk and then to think; and *Thinktalk* indicates a person whose habit is first to think and then to talk.

People who think while talking

Every family consists of people with one or the other of these two different kinds of thought processes. One person thinks and then talks; the other person talks and then thinks. It has often been observed that the ladies in a family can have the habit of talking and then thinking. If a lady wants to consider which household chores she needs to carry out, she does not think in her mind, rather, she thinks aloud. She may say, "Clothes need to be ironed, children have to be taken to school, breakfast isn't ready yet... when will all these things get done?" By verbalizing these matters, she is, in fact, searching for a solution. Thus, when a woman starts talking, she is thinking at the same time. If she is told, "Think first about a solution to your problem by yourself; think first then talk," she is not able to do so. She needs someone to listen to her, and by talking in front of that person she finds the solution to her problems. In other words, she is habituated to thinking aloud.

However, when a woman working at home thinks aloud, people around her may feel increased stress while listening to her. They develop the misunderstanding that their home is beset by a lot of problems. Meanwhile, unaware of the anxiety she creates, the think-aloud conversations continue: "Why is this thing left here? Can't you tidy up after you? The curtains must be cleaned. There is dust all over the floor. The trash needs taking out. What gift do we need to get for the wedding we have to attend?" The woman of the house carries on talking in this way, because she is of a talk-then-think nature.

When a talk-think man comes home, he is oppressed with thoughts, one after the other. He speaks out loud while thinking, "I'll bet the children have bunked off school and come home early, they use any excuse to take off. I've told them so many times to check their watches and do things on time, but they never listen." He then calls the children and admonishes them, "You'll find any excuse to quit school early. You always do this!" Hearing this, the children get upset and tell him, "But Dad, don't you have faith in us? That clock you are looking at stopped working a long time ago; we got home from school exactly on time."

To cover up his mistake, he then calls his wife and scolds her, "You don't attend to anything. You haven't noticed the clock at all; it stopped working ages ago. You're not paying attention to the household and you never know what the children are doing." Now the wife snaps back at the husband, "These days, it's you that aren't giving me any attention. You have responsibilities as well. But all you do is yell at me all the time." If, in one home, there are two think-aloud people, such scenes are bound to happen!

People who talk without thinking, or understanding, continually verbalize all the thoughts that appear in their minds, whether those are relevant or not. In the company of such people, others feel they are being accused by a harsh tongue. In fact, this isn't really so, because deliberate accusations would require prior thought. Such people are simply speaking their mind before they have time to think. Unfortunately, confusion and rumors abound in the environment of such people. In talk-think families, problems always crop up because no one thinks before they talk. Such people simply talk and talk wherever they go, as if they were a record constantly playing. When such people start speaking, they do not know when to stop.

People who talk after thinking

People who speak after thinking are the exact opposite of the above. They will always first think in their mind before speaking. Such people spend most of their time in their head, with their intellect. Such think-talk people may not talk at all, or very little. Often, others will have to wait for them to utter anything. When family members speak to a think-talk person, they will often find them lost in thoughts; if they do respond, it may be after a long while – which is very irritating for others.

When people exhibit either of these extremes, then talk-think people never think and think-talk people never talk. We must avoid both these types of extremes and make our responses appropriate by remaining at the center of both.

A husband and wife will often have different temperaments. The husband is frequently a think-then-talk person and the wife is often a talk-then-think person. This again is a cause for conflicts and problems between a couple because a single platform of communication does not exist between the two. This can have an impact on their lives and on those of their children.

To bring peace to a family, both husband and wife must understand each other's nature. Due to their different dispositions, their ways of thinking and conduct are different. The meaning of life for the husband and the wife will also appear different, and therefore they will lead their lives each according to their nature. When a man and a woman begin living together, due to these differences in nature and ways of thinking and acting, disagreements are bound to crop up between them. If the man understands these differences, then he will reduce his expectations that his wife must think like him. If the woman also understands these differences, then she will not expect her husband to always think as emotionally as her.

The other person is not like us. They have a different nature. We need to pay attention to this crucial fact. The root cause of fights in a family is that each member is unaware of the nature of the others. Each person's wish of the others is: "Be like me... think as I do, solve problems the way I do, keep things in their place as I do, speak to others as I do, think and talk as I do." However, when a new light appears in their relationships, they understand that '*Be like me*' is the source of all problems. This new insight can provide strength to their relationships.

After learning this truth, you need to avoid the extremes of both *talk-think* and *think-talk*. You should adopt a middle path by responding to all with understanding. Neither think then talk, nor talk then think; instead, always respond according to the need of the situation. Speak from your heart and seek to make your relationships complete.

15

*When the silence of completeness arises in relations,
the noise of incompleteness disappears.*

How to Make Your Relationships Complete

Speak your heart

When a sense of incompleteness takes hold in relationships, the peace of completeness vanishes. When people can convey what is in their hearts and make others understand what they mean, then they feel the joy of peace and silence. Not being able to speak their hearts, the storm of words rumbles incessantly inside them.

When you achieve completion or closure by saying what is in your heart, you feel satisfied and happy. You get the same satisfaction at the culmination of every task that is accomplished successfully. When work remains incomplete, you feel something inside is bothering you: this is called the sense of incompletion.

The sense of completion is when you finish something in the right manner using all your senses intelligently and with full focus. Your inner desire is completion in every aspect of life. If a task of yours is left incomplete, your thoughts repeatedly return to it. How many such matters are there in your life that are calling out to you because they are unfinished?

If you learn the art of completion in your life, then when you exit from this world, your passing will not be like that of so many people. Those who die with a sense of incompletion are pained by it. A man who is close to death calls all his relatives to his bedside, then says,

"If all of you are here, then who is managing the family business?" He is unable to relinquish his concerns because of the feeling of incompleteness regarding his business at this moment.

An individual with a long disagreement with someone might ask for forgiveness when on his deathbed. If he feels he has not helped someone, he may leave money for that person in his will. In his final moments, he recalls all those things not completed during his lifetime. When dying, people who have led incomplete lives think, "If only I had done these things when I had the time, then I would not be leaving this world with such remorse."

No one likes incompleteness in their life. Understand the importance of completion. From today, start completing all those things that are incomplete in your life. There will be many things which you do not realize are incomplete and you have not considered completing them. Examine all the activities that you carry out from morning to night, and you will realize that many remain unfinished. This is one of the reasons you get dreams at night. These incomplete tasks seek completion through your dreams. Ask yourself whether such incomplete matters induce peaceful sleep or destroy peaceful sleep. Do you wake in the morning rested, or do your thoughts and dreams disturb your sleep?

It is also important to make our relationships complete. In order to attain completeness in relations, it is essential to speak openly, using the appropriate words. Before seeking such completion, tell the concerned person, "I don't know how best to speak about the matter in my mind, so should I speak or should I keep it to myself?" When addressed in this way, the other person will likely want to be helpful and reply, "It's okay, you can say what you want, and however you wish."

To dissolve any discord between you and some relative or friend, open your heart to them. If there is something about someone lingering in your mind, tell that person: "There has been something in my mind for several days, which I haven't been able to mention. But, today, I wish to speak to you about it." Then begin with such words as: "I don't want to criticize you because I could be quite wrong, but I do want to give you my point of view in order to achieve closure." After saying this, you can speak about whatever was suppressed in your mind.

In this way, after achieving closure, you won't have to carry the issue around in your head. And you will no longer feel the need to be dishonest with that person or resort to unnecessary lies.

Everyone has different needs and desires that remain unfulfilled or incomplete. Simply complete them. When you learn the art of 'completion' or closure, your mind will stop running into the past or the future because it will find completeness in the present.

Let's suppose you had a fight with someone ten years back. Even today, you can go to that person and achieve completion by saying, "I did have negative emotions in my mind about you, but they are gone now. I am closing this issue. I do not want thoughts about the quarrel any longer. You can also tell me anything you wish, so you can achieve completion as well." In this way, you can offer the other person an opportunity to express their feelings also, so they too can feel the satisfaction of completeness. Whoever is complete, will complete others. Whoever is incomplete, will also keep others incomplete.

However, 'completion' does not only involve negative matters; positive things can be completed as well. If you like someone's qualities, convey this. Many people experience others' positive qualities all their lives, but are unable to admire them openly.

Suppose your feeling towards a co-worker is, "She works so well," but you have never told her. This feeling can also give you a sense of incompletion. Therefore, if you admire the qualities of a person, tell them about it. And if you don't like something about them, tell him about that also, but in appropriate words. This is how to carry out the process of completion. However, common sense should also be used in this process. Completion is not meant to hurt anyone and therefore it has to be done in a pleasant manner.

Henceforth, whenever you have a conversation with someone, at the end, ask yourself, "Was the dialogue we had today complete or not?" If you feel that it was not complete, then continue by saying, "If you felt bad about anything I said, please forgive me." If the conversation was difficult, it is important to ask the other person if they were upset. Hearing you, and seeing your completion, it is possible they may say, "Not at all! If I were in your place, I would have said the same thing." In this way, neither of you will retain any negative views about the other. You both can leave the meeting knowing it is complete.

By carrying out this process of completion or closure in your family too, these relationships will also be strengthened. The next section of this book is devoted to this subject.

How to Strengthen Relationships In The Family

16

Life is not about falling and recovering. It is about falling, recovering, and rising up – not empty-handed, but with a lesson.

HUSBAND-WIFE AND CHILDREN
The real meaning of marriage

Why were relationships originally created? The secret behind the creation of the institution of marriage is to make it possible to attain Self-Realization through the union of two people. Both husband and wife are supposed to be instrumental in each attaining the Ultimate Truth and discovering the true self.

This understanding has vanished in today's world. Today, people are still getting married, but this understanding is missing. Those who get married fight with each other just like kids. When they bear children, how will they raise them? Marriage is losing its meaning due to the disappearance of the real purpose of this sacred relationship between husband and wife.

With what purpose did God create the male and the female body? Who is getting married with whom and why? What is the purpose of human life on Earth? Marrying, bearing children, raising them, getting them married, taking care of their children, getting old, and dying… is this the only reason we were born?

The human body, be it male or female, is only a medium or a means; but we have become totally entangled in the body. Our entire life is spent indulging in sensual pleasures and illusory attractions. The body is a medium to be utilized in attaining Self-Realization. We have totally forgotten this fact. When will we fulfil our purpose of coming into this world?

People with no understanding of the Truth, and no one to impart understanding to them, get married and bear children. What will be the tendencies of these children? If those who are fighting like children bear children, what will be their children's future? It's unimaginable! Conflicts and disputes between husband and wife have a serious impact on their offspring.

> A husband was very angry with his wife and filed a court case against her. His wife allegedly used to treat him like a dog and hence he wanted a divorce. The judge asked the wife, "Do you treat your husband like a dog?" The wife was annoyed and shouted at her husband, "Okay, I won't treat you like a dog anymore, just as soon as you stop barking at me."

One can easily identify the superficial causes of conflicts, and their temporary solutions, such as buying a present to calm the argument… offering an apology… using the word 'please'… or agreeing that one's behavior was wrong. These steps can put an immediate stop to a conflict, but the deeper causes may be understood only much later.

Each incident in life offers an experience; and we have to learn to benefit from our experiences. Imagine you are walking along the street and suddenly fall down. You will first try to recover and get up. But do not get up empty handed. While rising, look for any coins (lessons) that may be lying around, and if there are any, do pick them up. There is something beneficial for you to gain from every experience. If fights are occurring in your family, that too is a learning experience. Tension in a relationship is also a learning experience. What are you learning from it? What lessons are you picking up from these experiences before rising up? If you do not learn from them, then these fights will continue all your life.

If your children grow up in an environment where conflicts regularly take place, then they will develop complexes – of either inferiority or superiority. Children who develop an inferiority complex consider themselves lesser than others. Those with a superiority complex consider themselves to be smarter than others. Both kinds of children are, in fact, ill. If the world gets such sick children, it is hard to imagine what the future of such children, or our own future will be. We should also consider the future of society, the nation, and ultimately the world. When these children grow up and bear their own children, will this world be healthy?

Every husband and wife should contemplate together what education they should give to their children so that they have a bright future. The seeds you sow in your children will bear sweet fruits for you too. Hence, whatever deeds you perform and whatever decisions you make in the family, do it with understanding. If parents are already well-tuned to each other, they will know when it is essential to scold a child and when that child needs love and affection. There would then be no clashes in the family. Only when both the husband and wife play the right role, at the right time, will the child receive the right upbringing.

To assist this, the husband–wife team should create a communication platform amongst themselves. They should decide beforehand that when one of them makes a mistake, can the other one point out the mistake or not. They should communicate daily with each other using the right language. In this way, both can openly discuss the happenings of the day, mistakes that were made, distractions that appeared, and how similar events should be handled in the future. If this kind of discussion, with an exchange of thoughts, takes place on a regular basis within the family, then a beautiful communication platform between the couple will be created.

Both husband and wife should be clear that the experiences for which they have come to Earth are of utmost importance. Both should help each other and be instrumental for each other in gaining the experience of 'being' for which they have been born as a human being. If both are aware of this and prepared for it, then the love that develops between the two would be real love. Real love is that love which is beyond love and hatred. It is devoid of deceit, jealousy, and ego. It is unconditional, selfless, and everlasting. Such love will have a tremendously positive effect on their children.

Such successful couples are the last hope for changing this world. If the world is to be changed, then first each parent should be given the right direction. Each parent has to become a complete person. This means they should be the one who strikes a chord between spiritual and worldly life; the one who is neither an ascetic nor just a householder, but reflects the best qualities of both; and the one who happily performs all worldly duties but never forgets the Truth or the ultimate purpose of life. Such successful couples can properly guide their children. The husband and wife can help each other to attain that Experience of 'being' for which they have come to Earth. This is the purpose of relationships. Make every relationship, including those with your children, instrumental in the right way to fulfil this purpose.

It is often seen that, instead of providing correct understanding, parents hand their children their own crutches. Their children then walk on these ready-made crutches for life. Parents have had some bitter-sweet life experiences, with the result that they label the world and its people as bad. They clutch onto these experiences, and their opinions, and eventually pass them on to their children. How will such children progress in life when they only reflect their parents' perspective?

What is the truth? Is the world actually bad? Are people bad? The same world that appears bad to some, appears good to others. We should give freedom to our children to form their opinions from their own perspective and experiences. Parents should not impose their own beliefs on their children. Let the children decide their own path. Do help them to choose, but do not impose your decisions on them. In this way, give them a new life, a new light, and then together plan your life.

17

*The family foundation becomes strong
when it is supported not by one but by all family members.
No external enemy can weaken that foundation.*

GET TOGETHER AND MAKE PLANS FOR YOUR LIFE

Make a group in your family

All family members should be responsible for the family. Placing the entire foundation of the family in the hands of one person is harmful for that person and eventually for the entire family. When the foundation of the family is jointly shared by all family members, that foundation becomes strong. Nobody from outside can then shake that foundation. Come, let us get together in the family and make plans for our life and for exploring the potential for unlimited joy.

In order to fortify the family's foundation, create a Family Growth Group. The group may consist of all the family members: husband, wife, sons, daughters, brothers, sisters and others if they are close. Working as a group in a family produces strong results because the family members not only have faith in one another, but also love each other. This group should meet weekly or twice a month to discuss how the family can progress in every aspect of life. Such a family group can lead to happiness and contentment.

The family is a platform in which you can come together and make plans for your life. Individuals who have chosen their life partner with understanding will welcome the support of their partner in this way. The power of a group that includes not only husband and wife, or father and mother, but other family members as well can invoke spiritual powers at home. This is the greatest power for attaining true love, happiness, and understanding in relationships.

By forming a growth group in the family, sympathy, love, and faith towards each other is intensified. This state can provide love, happiness, and success to each person. Love between husband and wife is generated and they feel encouraged to willingly help each other. Such love is capable of changing a person's desires and direction. It is the power of love that can help an individual get rid of all addictions and bad habits. Bound by love, a person can face the greatest of hardships.

By forming a group in the family, all family members can easily converse about mutual progress. Such daily conversations can inspire each to move towards their goal. If family members form a common communication platform and create good rapport among themselves, then the chances of conflicts in the family will reduce or cease. Noting the abundance of love, life, and laughter in your family, friends and neighbors may also be inspired to form such family growth groups. In this way, a group starting with a husband and wife leading to happiness in the family, can spread to society, the nation, and eventually the entire universe.

Seeing one happy family, many other happy families will be created. If the maximum potential of happiness is explored and enhanced by one family, then these happy vibrations can spread exponentially across the universe. How wonderful that would be. No longer would there be war and unrest. Each one of us would get the full opportunity to open up, blossom, and be happy. In this way, a family growth group can influence the world to change and explore higher possibilities.

A family growth group can help spread thoughts of the same level of consciousness among all members of the family. This is exactly what will instigate cooperation, compassion, mutual love, and the feeling of support from each other during difficult times.

If you need multiple hands for work, express appreciation rather than criticism. If you can get good results with honey, then why use poison! By appreciating each other, we help to enhance each other's qualities. In this new life plan, we need to get together to form a higher communication platform. In the next chapter, we construct this platform.

18

When the highest possibility of happiness is explored and achieved by one family, its vibrations will spread all over the universe. How beautiful the universe would then be!

HOW TO BUILD THREE HIGHER PLATFORMS FOR COMMUNICATION IN THE FAMILY

Foundation for better relationships

All the parts of a machine, whether small or large, are merely parts. They do not function for themselves; rather the machine functions through them. In ignorance, these parts feel that they are working for themselves and have a separate existence from the machine. But you know this is not so, because you can see the machine functioning as a whole. Drawing parallels from this example, it becomes clear that the whole world is one family. Out of ignorance, individual human beings claim to be working independently for themselves because they are unable to see the whole picture. In fact, it is the universal being that is functioning collectively through all the bodies.

Almost everybody in the world gets the thought of helping others. If one person stops getting such thoughts and ceases to help, someone else starts getting those thoughts and takes over the role. If a mother abandons her newborn baby and leaves it to be found, someone else will take over its nurturing. In this way the entire world, which is one big family, is being taken care of.

Your family, with all its members, is like a book comprising multiple sections. The various sections of this book need to be bound by the thread of common understanding. A platform is the foundation of common understanding that provides the binding of all the family members together as a single unit. When this thread of understanding begins to bind your family together, you will witness miracles. With the formation of such a platform, true love, that was always present but veiled by the dust of doubts and distrust, will begin to shine forth.

In a global sense, when people from different religions, castes, and belief systems begin to come together on a common platform which is founded on higher understanding, then merchants of violence who infuse terror in the name of religious differences will cease to exist. Those who seize power by selling hatred in the name of religion will disappear. The need of today is not for a new religion, but for the sacred thread of higher understanding that binds all religions together.

This is a higher vision, the achievement of which requires each one of us to start functioning consciously out of love. Any effort towards this vision begins with the family, which is the most fundamental unit of human society. We need to deeply contemplate what the words 'I' and 'we' mean, and who is actually functioning through 'us'. The more we contemplate this, the more we can be centered on 'we' (our family) by growing beyond the limitations of the individual 'I'.

If you want the support of all family members in this endeavor, if you wish to open up and realize the collective potential of your family, if you wish to increase love, joy, and laughter in your life, then you will need to build a 'higher platform' for family communication. If there has never been such a platform in your family, if all family members have not thought collectively about such matters, then the time has come for the whole family to read this book and start to think in a new way.

Usually, it is only when arguments begin in a relationship that people start thinking about building a common communication platform. This is akin to digging a well after you feel thirsty. If the well is dug in advance, then water will be available whenever required.

Prevention is better than cure. It is better to start exercising now to keep your body healthy than to start after falling ill. Once you are ill and weak, you will not be strong enough for exercise. So you should start well before you fall sick. You will stay fit, prevent repetitive illness, and recover quickly even if you do fall ill. Similarly, you should make a higher platform for communication well before disputes or problems arise within the family. When the level of consciousness of all family members is high, get together and build at least three different platforms.

FIRST PLATFORM: WITH YOURSELF

For the first platform, you need to sit in solitude with a diary and contemplate: "What are the things I can do to spread happiness in the family? Which habits of mine are troublesome for my family members?" Note down all such points in your diary.

You need to eliminate all bad habits and behavioral patterns from your mind and body. Perhaps, you are hot tempered and get angry at every trivial issue. If this is the case, then contemplate all the ill-effects your anger has caused in the past and those it could cause in the future. Perhaps something was not done to your wishes, perhaps someone disregarded your advice, perhaps someone did not give you the respect you thought you deserved, all of which led to resentment and poor relations. Write down those incidents and bring to light the behavioral patterns you have that are detrimental to harmony within your family. Reflect on how you can overcome them.

This is the right time for you to do something to bring joy into your family. To establish this first platform, decide to eliminate your own shortcomings so that all family members can come together on a common platform. Get rid of your shortcomings out of love and not out of compulsion. If you are able to build such a platform with yourself then this will be your biggest gift to your family.

SECOND PLATFORM: WITH YOUR FAMILY

The second platform needs to be built jointly amongst all the members of your family. Such a platform for communication needs to be established on mutually agreed terms and with wholehearted consent. Again, all members of the family should understand and be committed to building such a platform out of love rather than compulsion.

Before any clashes take place, family members should decide in advance how they should deal with each other during any disturbing incident or periods of stress. Discussion and agreement should be reached on such details as: How others should behave with us when we feel angry; how to deal with someone else when they are angry; whether or not to intervene in an argument; and what words to use to avoid inflaming a situation. Collective thought should be given to: What to do if the habits of one person trouble another; how to solve family problems together; what role each member should play; and how often meetings should be held to discuss and reset the platform of common understanding. The type of problems requiring agreed procedures could be financial, social, children-related, or even the temperament of a family member.

You can sit together to discuss matters and reach appropriate solutions. After consulting with each other, you can even decide upon gestures and reminders that can be used to alert each other when potential clashes arise.

Have you ever seen huge flocks of birds circling the sky together in fascinating formations, and wondered how they move together without colliding, despite flying so close to each other? They do not have traffic signals, yet they are able to produce such brilliant expressions of teamwork and coordination using a sophisticated signaling mechanism between them. As members of a family, you ought to discuss and agree upon such signaling mechanisms to alert each other and avoid clashes in various situations.

For example, a family can make use of the term 'spic-and-span'. There would be a common understanding that whenever any member of the family utters 'spic-and-span', every member of the family will stop whatever they are doing and spend the next ten minutes tidying up the house. This would avoid pressure on just one member to do all the cleaning and ensure the house always looks in good order.

The Family Mission Statement

As mentioned earlier, if the family can be likened to a book, it will be helpful to jointly contemplate and agree upon a mission statement for the family. It need not be a very sophisticated or fancy title. It can be something as simple as 'Whatever we do, we do it with a smile' or '1 + 1 = 11' indicating that your family has far greater total potential working collectively than the cumulative potential of individuals. The statement can also be a reminder of harmony such as, 'We're a family that sows the seeds of patience and lives peacefully under the tree of love.'

Once you have decided upon your family's mission statement, you need to put a system in place that will remind all family members about your common purpose. For this, you can discuss creative ideas for suitable gestures. For example, clutching both the hands together can be an indication of unity and harmony. This will serve as a reminder to other members.

The family should also have a bookmark, which indicates how far they have progressed on the path of their common mission. If the family is frequently returning to the same chapters of their book, that is, going through the same unpleasant experiences repeatedly, then they are not making progress. Instead, they are remaining stationary or slipping backwards on their mission. As a bookmark tells us how far we have progressed reading a book, the family bookmark in the form of sense of purpose will constantly remind the family for progressing consistently and ceaselessly.

Different Viewpoints Supporting a Common Vision

When two managers in a company are discussing the execution of a project, one asks the other, "How will you go about it?" The other replies, "I will do it this way." The first person says, "I would do it the same way too." The second person exclaims, "Then why are we both working on the same project?!" If both are going to function in the same manner, then they should work on different projects. It is only when there is a variety of views that something new can be invented. To invent something new in the household too, the different views of wife, husband, and children can be combined, provided they have the same progressive goal. The constructive product of different viewpoints can bring forth an altogether new dimension.

Each person has a different nature, different viewpoint on life, different preferences, and a unique thought process. Yet each can contribute towards a common vision for the family. Having a variety of perspectives is actually a strength that can be leveraged to make collective progress in a common direction.

Every family member should understand that they need to welcome and accommodate all viewpoints from the other family members. Nothing in this world is useless. Even the most illogical perspective can actually serve as a bridge for growth.

People can be classified into two categories based on their mental faculties. Those with a left-brain predominance are logical and methodical in their thought process. They can plan meticulously. Those with a right-brain predominance are creative, intuitive, and can work wonders with colors and pictures, though their thought processes may appear illogical. If both these categories of people exist within a family, it is indeed a blessing if their strengths can be identified and harnessed together. When both these kinds of people work together constructively, then the result will be that of a Bright brain that can produce a remarkable eureka effect!

Meeting Culture

In order to establish a platform for communication, all members of your family need to subscribe to a meeting culture. Family meetings should be held at regular intervals based on joint consent. Such meetings should be used to discuss the common mission of the family, as well as steps that need to be undertaken to make progress. 'Soft' issues can be discussed by seeking the honest opinions of all family members. The key here is that each family member should participate wholeheartedly out of love, and be receptive to the others.

If you are attempting to introduce meeting culture in your family for the first time, it would be useful to do so only at an opportune time, that is, when all members are in a relatively good mood. The family can also choose to meet at a place away from the daily environment, perhaps a picnic spot, for the first few meetings.

Use of Safeguard Words in Communication

An important element of communication is the use of safeguard words when talking from the heart with a family member or anyone else. Safeguard words are used to ensure that we do not hurt others' feelings while communicating what we want. The advance message you should convey is that you will continue to love the person regardless of whatever you are about to discuss; your words will not dent your love or respect in any way.

Once this is clarified, you must also say that your statements are just your opinion. It is helpful to say, "This is what I feel from my limited perspective, but I may be wrong." In this way, the recipient will not feel offended and will be able to receive you positively. Lastly, when you are expressing what you feel, you should be aware that you are stating only your own opinion and not proclaiming the universal truth. This should be reflected not only in your words but also in your tone. This topic is also addressed in detail in Chapter 15.

Use of Footnotes for Contemplation

Footnotes are brief lines of description in the page footer that explain words that are referenced on the page. Just like footnotes, each family member needs to note down those words or phrases that irritate or disturb them. Whenever you hear such words or phrases in conversation within the family, you should shift your focus to your footnotes and reflect upon why these words or phrases disturb you. The very act of shifting focus helps you to detach yourself from the scene and avoid an impulsive reaction. If you contemplate carefully, you will realize that no incident by itself is disturbing. It is the thoughts that are triggered within you that cause the disturbance.

For example, suppose you feel sad when thinking, "I don't have a car." You may then consider, "But what has a car to do with happiness or worthiness?" You may answer with a response such as, "People who have a car are respected." This you counter with, "But many without a car are still respected." Then you continue, "But people with a car can make meetings on time." And you counter, "But not all people who drive cars are punctual." In this way, you can analyze the thoughts that influence your feelings, and unearth the false notions that are present in your mind.

All members of the family need to learn this art of self-introspection. On most occasions, doubting our own thoughts, instead of doubting people around us, can deliver a pleasant surprise.

Some tips for establishing the platform for communication

If you are unaware of doing something wrong, then an indication from another family member will immediately bring you back to awareness. This can prevent ill-effects like stresses and strains in relationships, or pollution of the family environment.

If someone in the family is already tense, pointing out any mistake may make them doubly upset. To avoid this, while building the family platform, consider agreeing upon a commonly understood signal, which will act as a reminder without causing additional upset.

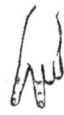

Remember that when advising someone about any bad habit, we can unconsciously begin to criticize them. This can result in increasing anger and a retaliatory response. So care needs to be taken whenever pointing out poor behavior. Even one word said lovingly can work as a reminder and produce a calming effect. Creating gestures and considering your responses will change your direction and that of your family for the better.

Some gestures that can be used as reminders are shown in the adjoining images.

THIRD PLATFORM: WITH CHILDREN

A platform needs to be created through daily communication with children from their early childhood. Children should observe and learn the meeting culture in their family. They should see that collective progress is the family's topmost priority. If a child notes that matters of progress are discussed in their home, then its full potential can be realized.

Children's familiarity with the progressive outlook of the family will involve an understanding of how each task can be performed in a better and more efficient manner; how mutual relations and communication can be improved; awareness of the feelings and thoughts of others; and the benefits of sharing knowledge on how to better perform any activity. If children are party to such discussions in regular family meetings, they will be able to understand the meeting training culture.

It is the parents' duty to openly converse with their children, and give them the opportunity to freely express their thoughts, problems, and experiences. If the elders simply shout orders then children will become confused. Each child will feel happier when included in the family mission rather than just obeying instructions. If the benevolent objective of the mission is visualized to children then they will willingly cooperate and contribute. Therefore, sufficient time should be spent with children to explain the common mission of the family in simple terms that they understand, such as, "We want to bring love, joy, and peace to the family."

When children are allowed to contribute in family meetings, you will be surprised by the originality of their creative input. Children should have faith that their parents wish them well, and that if they speak the truth they will not be punished or reprimanded. Parents must exercise patience while listening to their children. Listen silently without reacting impulsively. Tell them, "We will not interrupt you. Just speak your heart. Feel absolutely free to tell us whatever is in your mind."

When children are called to participate in a meeting, they should not feel their parents want to reform them, or that the objective is to get them to 'improve'. In that case, they will not enjoy participating. Children should be respected as individuals. They have their own identity, emotions, opinions, and desires, and a right to express their feelings. Parents who wish to build a platform of communication with their children, should solve their children's problems in discussion with them. Children should be encouraged to express their opinion on at least minor family problems. If they are able to think about a given problem and give their opinion, this will help develop decision-making ability and survival skills.

If children do not get good grades in their studies, parents often express their dissatisfaction angrily. Due to lack of awareness, parents may even give their children the impression that they are 'good-for-nothing' and 'inferior' in comparison to others. This can have a devastating long-term impact on a child's confidence and cause a severe dent in self-esteem. Instead of criticizing children, parents should have a calm and loving conversation with them, such as, "Tell us what difficulties you have. We can jointly find a solution. All problems can be solved. Don't be anxious, instead let's resolve to overcome this. We love you regardless." Generating such faith in children is vital. This assures them that you are supporting them. Faith is the foundation that strengthens relationships. Your children will then be able to openly share their problems with you, so that you can find solutions together and implement them.

All parents should understand that children are not their property; they are not their owners. We are all instrumental in each other's growth and ability to rise higher. Make this third communication platform for your children with this view in mind.

Responsibility for Sowing the Seeds of Progress

Realizing one's responsibility, one should make a fresh beginning with one's own family. Has your family invited the collective growth that is described here? Or is progress still not discussed in your family? It is easy to wait for others to make a start. It requires genuine love and a sense of purpose to seize the initiative. You have to seize the initiative because it is your role. As it is you who are reading these lines, the responsibility is yours.

The human body has many essential parts. The eyes, ears, hands, legs, stomach, brain, heart, and other organs each perform key functions. However, if the eyes were to say, "This body has hands, legs, stomach, heart, and so many other parts, but I am the only one who has to see." Do the eyes ever complain, "Why don't the hands see for a change?" The eyes clearly know that visual perception is their job. In the same way, the family too is like a single body with a collective conscious principle. Various members of the family perform different functions such as organizer, sponsor, worker, thinker, director, and so on. It is the job of the heart of the family to ensure that the essence of the family shines forth. It is the heart of the family that binds the family together and ensures that everyone moves in a common direction of growth. You have to own up to this responsibility for your family.

Make the members of your family a party to the family mission statement so that they feel responsible and work towards it. If the end result is visualized as a great scene of joy and harmony, and one feels good just hearing about it, then when it begins to happen in the family, how blissful it would be! Everyone will prepare for it, be they adults or children.

Soon, you will find that arguments and differences that used to take months to get resolved will pass in a day. Many disturbing incidents that occurred due to lack of awareness and understanding of each other will simply vanish from your everyday life.

In the future, many families will be able to declare that they have learnt how a family can progress continuously and consistently. Continuous 'in-life' training for harmony and collective growth will become an integral part of family life. Every family member will sincerely review their progress in the current year and eagerly discuss the next steps to be taken for improvements in the following year. The family will measure its progress in terms of qualities that have been developed individually as well as collectively.

When children hear such talk of progress from their infancy, when they find that their parents keep discussing how to further improve their functioning as a collective unit, even though everything is already going well, then the seeds of growth will be sown. It is these seeds that we have to sow for the future. It is these seeds, in the form of progressive children, that will grow up and contribute to the larger family on the planet, thereby bringing about a global revolution and making each home a heaven.

19

Relationships filled with love indicate abundant happiness.
Relationships devoid of love only make noise like empty vessels.

How To Make Your Home A Heaven
Plan love and understanding for all

Anybody can make their environment a heaven. Those who spend their days at work, can make their workplace a heaven. Homemakers who spend their time at home can make their home a heaven.

If people do not like to return to their homes, it is because they perceive their homes to be hell. If a husband is apprehensive that he will hear only complaints when he reaches home, then he will prefer to remain away from the home as long as possible. He will talk to anybody to waste time before returning, because he is tormented by the complaints and accusations he receives at home.

This can be the story in many homes today, because the lady of the house does not understand that her complaints and suspicions make her home a living hell. If such a lady were to think differently and consider how to make a communication platform in her family, then soon her home would transform into a heaven. She could decide and plan when she would discuss each matter of concern with her husband. If the family members scheduled a time to sort out all their complaints once a week, the home environment would improve immensely. Daily complaints lead to a habit of complaining, and the person who must listen to these complaints becomes desensitized. Avoid all of this if you want to make your home a warm and loving place.

Women can make their homes a heaven because it is usually they who have the responsibility of taking care of every member of the family. To create this heaven, they should be aware of everything going on in the house. What is the physical and mental state of each family member when they return home? Do they arrive hungry? Do they return troubled or tired from office or school? All such things should be considered and understood by the homemaker of the family, and some preparations can be made in advance. If someone comes home tired, then something can be planned beforehand to ease their fatigue. If such things are actually taken care of, then arriving home will feel like heaven to those returning.

If the homemaker is herself upset, then she will be unable to make her home a heaven. Instead, she will transmit her own troubles to others. Therefore, the rest of the family should sit down and decide how they can help their mother or wife in the domestic work. At least once a month, all the family can help in the household cleaning. If each person also keeps everything in the house in an orderly manner, items can be easily located when needed, and work can be completed on time. All will then feel the home to be a heavenly place. If everything is left scattered around the house, then it will feel like a hell. Thus, to ensure the home maintains a healthy and heavenly state, all members should list the daily chores and divide them amongst themselves. This way, no single person will be burdened with all the work, and each gets a small number of chores to complete.

No more Mother-in-law or Daughter-in-law

Your family should be an inspiration to others by showing how each home can be a temple that celebrates love. As a girl hugs her mother, after her marriage she can hug her mother-in-law too. If she fears her mother-in-law, then she should put an end to her! She can do this simply by treating her mother-in-law as her mother instead. With no more mother-in-law, there will be no more mother-in-law–daughter-in-law problems. Hugging is also a type of communication. When a person feels unable to express their feelings in words, then hugging is the best form of expression. This way, any fears or apprehensions disappear, and all can join forces to make their home a heaven.

Where a mother-in-law and a daughter-in-law hug each other, where youngsters and elders respect each other, where elders bless the youngsters, where everything is kept in order, where people join hands to work, where members eat and celebrate festivals together with true understanding, where relationships are free from deceit, ego, obsessions, suspicions, presumptions, and complaints, where family members are aware of the stress levels of each other, where people can speak openly and sort out misunderstandings, where people can speak their hearts in a soft tone, where three communication platforms have been built within the family, where everyone understands each other – there is love, life, and laughter in such relationships and such a home is indeed a heaven.

TRASFORM YOURSELF, OTHERS, AND THE WORLD

20

Do not focus your attention on the little black spot that mars the pure white sheet; focus on the whiteness of the sheet instead.

MAGICAL STEP 1: WE BECOME WHAT WE FOCUS ON
Develop qualities through the art of observation

To understand the real nature of relationships, you must first learn the art of observation. If you are asked whether you know what observation means, you will reply that, of course, you know what it means and how to practice it. For most people, observation simply means looking closely at things. Observing objects is a concept we are all familiar with, because everyone does it, and the world could not function without it. Yet, the true 'art of observation' is no common or ordinary faculty, it should be studied and valued as an extremely important tool of human life.

Every day people are observing something. But if you ask them what they are observing, you will find that most of the time they are busy observing other people's flaws. Ask them what they know about the people around them and they will fluently narrate others' imperfections and problems. People derive pleasure from probing others' weaknesses. The focus is nearly always on the bad and negative. No doubt they are keenly observing, but they are mostly observing things that they do not need.

Even a child observes. He watches how to walk, talk, and bend down. He keenly observes how to smile, how to keep things in place, and how to eat. Without even formal education, he easily succeeds in learning everything – just through observation. What does the mathematics of observation have to say? Surprisingly, the common man uses only one-thousandth of his observation powers, and yet he learns so much. Humans are capable of observing and duplicating anything.

So, do you want to put your faculty of observation to the test? Try your hand at the following exercises.

1. Jot down everything you can remember about your own wrist-watch. Do not look at your watch, just start writing. Describe the casing of your watch, the color of the dial, the type of numerals at each hour, the divisions between the hours, the brand name engraved on the face, and any other details you can recall. When you have finished, check the accuracy of your list. Now you will know the capacity of your observation.

2. Take a walk along a street that you regularly visit. This time be more observant and draw your attention to every building, shopfront, advertisement, traffic sign, tree, plant-pot, and anything else in view. You will be surprised to find that when you observe with attention, you will see many things you had not noticed before.

Observation – the greatest tool

Man has been blessed with the power of observation. It is at work incessantly, and you cannot easily stop it. Hence, the wise thing to do is to ensure you use this great tool correctly at all times. The faculty of observation works automatically, and the results are stored in memory cells for your use. You are bound to use whatever is stored. Understand this through the following examples.

1. When your friend sings a song, soon you too start humming the same tune, even if you have not consciously listened to it.

2. If your friend always wears a broad smile, then observing this face regularly you get into the habit of smiling the same way.

3. If you are impressed by the way your favorite movie star walks, you are likely to develop a similar walk without deliberate imitation.

4. If your friend has a habit of cracking jokes, you will develop the same habit too.
5. If your brother likes to whistle while taking a shower, you may start doing the same.
6. If your father makes a strange sound when sipping his tea, you may unconsciously start following his example.
7. If your mother makes hand gestures while speaking, you too develop the same gestures.
8. If your friend always says "Oops!! Sorry!" after a slip of the tongue, you may develop this habit too.

Deciphering how observation works

From the above examples, you can understand how we acquire habits, how we develop many of our qualities, and how our character takes shape. We do not have to toil for this. Most of this happens with very little effort because the tool of observation functions unceasingly. The distinctive feature of this tool is that whatever you focus upon, you will potentially assimilate – even if you are focused on a practice you do not like. Hence, you need to be careful, because if this tool is used without awareness you may develop negative habits. The following examples illustrate how this happens.

1) Suppose your friend has a nail-biting habit and you regularly warn her that it is unhealthy. Gradually, when you are not thinking, you start biting your nails too.
2) A woman hates her mother-in-law always shouting at her. After some time, however, she finds herself doing the same with her own children.
3) You dislike the elaborate gestures your friend makes during arguments. But then you realize that you have started making the same hand movements when you argue.
4) You agree that smoking is a bad habit, yet you continue to smoke. This habit has been acquired, and continues to be reinforced, by observing others smoking.

5) You dislike bad handwriting but observe your colleagues hurriedly scrawling written notes. Soon you too copy their habit of writing poorly.

The above examples show that you do what you observe, and the faculty of observation is the basis for forming habits. Your behavior, when talking, walking, eating, sleeping, working, or doing anything else, is based on what you observe. Using this tool, you can learn many things, in little time and with minimum effort. Therefore, beware of what you observe. *Observe only those habits that you wish to inculcate. Pay no attention to those you do not wish to follow.*

If put to proper use, the power of observation can bring about astonishing results. Use it for your benefit; not for developing unwanted habits. Do not worry about what your friends think of you. If necessary, change your company for your own benefit, because only in the right personal company will you get to observe the qualities and habits you ought to emulate. If you want to be a businessman, then seek the company of businessmen and not of doctors. If you want to become a teacher, then make friendships with teachers and not musicians. If you want to be an artist, then don't spend your time with lawyers. And if you want to become a world class sportsperson, then don't waste your time in the company of politicians.

Assess your circle of friends. If required, make way for new friends in your life. It is quite possible that you will face challenges in letting go of your old company of friends. They may even call you selfish. But do not succumb to such influences. Without wealth, how will you help your poor friends? In order to acquire wealth, you must seek the company of the rich, and learn their methods of earning money. As the old saying goes: *'If you want to help the poor, then you cannot afford to be poor yourself.'* You can set an example to your disadvantaged friends that they too can become wealthy – in knowledge, if not always in finance. Prove this by becoming wealthy yourself and later on they will praise you.

If you become an outstanding example, your former friends will seek to follow your footsteps. But first you must take care of your own well-being, only then will you be able to help society. Therefore, be selfish in the right sense, help yourself so that later you can really help others. You must learn to swim before you can save a drowning man. Does this not make sense?

Now you are on an important mission. In order to progress in life, you are about to enter new company. At this stage, you have to cross one more milestone. Let us suppose that you are an ordinary student with average intelligence. You have established a friendship with a bright student in your class and started frequenting his home. But after a while, you find it difficult to mix with him because of your different attitudes and habits. Your new friend shares his skills with you – his study strategies, his lecture notes, as well as the excellent grades he has received. In contrast, you lag behind in your work because you have been watching television or wasting time with other friends. As a result, you are unable to discuss your studies with him and you feel inferior and discouraged. Even so, you should not leave his company; you must continue being his friend. Slowly, your awareness will increase, then you too will decide that you need to study and finish your assignments instead of wasting time in unproductive activities. You will now feel confident and assured in the beneficial company of an accomplished friend.

A dull student will always feel most comfortable in the company of those who frivolously waste their time. This is because such people talk the same language. They will discuss movies they have watched, bands that they listen to, or TV talent shows as if they were giving 'expert' commentary. How can such company benefit anyone or stimulate any kind of positive growth? Therefore, assess your personal company, and decide to *always be with people who are ahead of you.* This change will trigger considerable improvements in your life.

If you are intent on climbing a mountain, be careful not to shake hands with those who are climbing down. It is difficult to climb up, but easy to climb down. The natural inclination of human nature is always towards the easier path. One cannot expect a comfort-loving person to achieve challenging goals. Therefore, you need to inculcate the habit of challenging your limitations and breaking out of your self-imposed comfort zone.

Influence of Company

When hydrogen is combined with oxygen, it produces water. But when hydrogen is combined with chlorine, it produces hydrochloric acid. Simply by changing its company, the same hydrogen gas transforms into a substance of totally opposite nature. We all know that water is indispensable for life, whereas acid can be used to seriously harm life. Hydrogen itself is neutral, but its behavior changes according to the element with which it is combined. Consider the reasons we have people with criminal dispositions in our society. Were they born criminals? No. They were brought up in surroundings where pick-pocketing, robbery, fraud, and even murder were the order of the day. Eventually they adopted those habits.

You therefore need to purposefully seek the company of those of a higher caliber. You may initially face some resistance. A rich man rarely befriends a poor man, and a manager would not wish close association with a simple clerk. But if you sincerely approach people of higher caliber, acknowledging their importance and influence, their resistance will gradually fade away. Even in colleges, the distinction between clever and dull students at the beginning of the year gradually changes into mutual friendships.

You seek the company of successful people because you want to observe their behavior. You want to understand their know-how and what makes them excel in their field. And you succeed in doing so only because you actually want to observe them. At this point, you need to fully understand the principle of observation: *You observe only what you want to observe.*

Let us get some clarity about this principle through some examples.

1) Members of a family are waiting at a bus stop. A shop in a nearby building available for rent catches the attention of the father. The mother is scrutinizing the clothes displayed

in a dress shop window. The elder son is interested in the movie posters on a bill-board. And the youngest is engrossed in watching a flock of pigeons and thinking, "I wish I could catch one and take it home." In this manner, people observe only what they want to observe.

2) A woman is watching news on a television channel. Her husband walks in and asks her about the latest news. But her response is a simple stare because she has been studying the appearance of the newsreader, not listening to the news.

3) A rich man gets richer because he sees only the abundant inflow of money. He expects to see this as a habitual sight, and with this self-confidence he thus grows richer. Another man focuses only on his dearth of money. From the day he gets his pay check he thinks only about his debts, bills, and deficit at the month's end. And his unchanging life is proof of his wrong focus.

4) Consider the life of vagabonds. They live by the roadside. They are born there, work there, eat there, and even celebrate their weddings on the pavements. Eventually they breathe their last on the pavements too. Since childhood, they have watched this kind of living under open skies, so they never even think of owning a house. This is the only reason they have such a lifestyle.

Reading these examples, you may ask: "How can a poor man become wealthy if he does not have the money to observe an abundance of wealth?" It is a sensible question, but if the poor man can feel and express happiness at the wealth acquired by others, and be truly happy for them, then he too can become rich. *Do not be envious of others' wealth; instead appreciate them for earning it.* If the poor man is able to change his pattern of thinking and admire the rich instead of envying them, after some time and reflection he will certainly be able to acquire wealth of his own.

The Way People Observe

Now that you have learnt different aspects of observation, you have to master this art. It is essential to train yourself in 'self-observation' too. And you also have to develop the skill of observing all the positive things around you.

> Two friends take refuge under a large tree to escape the sun on a hot afternoon. Looking at the tree, one of them says, "This tree is useless. It doesn't have any fruit." Agreeing with him, his friend says, "It doesn't even bear any flowers." A traveler, sitting under the same tree, overhears this conversation and interrupts by saying, "You are not looking at things correctly. Sitting under the canopy of this tree, you should be appreciating the cool shade it offers; instead you just highlight its deficiencies. Observe what you benefit from this tree, instead of what you don't."

This viewpoint is absolutely correct. It is only by observing from a positive perspective that you can enhance the quality of your observations. The example above illustrates that if we think negatively then we will always observe the negative aspects of everything. We will fail to see the positive and beautiful things that surround us. Therefore, train yourself to see the positive, and enrich your observation capability.

A small dark stain on a clean, white table cloth will always catch our attention. We completely ignore the pure whiteness of the cloth and just focus on the stain. Hence, we need to train our eyes to always first observe the positive aspects of anything. It is rightly said that even a broken watch shows the correct time twice a day!

You too can master the skill of observation. And you do not have to work hard. You only have to change the direction of the way you look, think, and judge. You will then be able to effortlessly inculcate good qualities. Thus, the first magical step enables you to acquire virtues through the art of observation, while through the second step you will learn how to benefit others with your whole heart.

21

*Even one word of appreciation
can become the source of inspiration for someone.*

MAGICAL STEP 2: APPRECIATE GENEROUSLY
How to encourage the best qualities in others

In this chapter, you will learn how you can be a catalyst in benefiting others. Do not be apprehensive about giving or sharing with others, it won't cost you anything. What is it that you have to give? You have to give appreciation to others from the bottom of your heart and with faith. You may not feel the need to appreciate others, but in this chapter you are going to learn how even a small act of sincere appreciation can bring about a big change in your relationships. You may already have observed many good qualities in your relatives, friends, and colleagues, now it is essential that you communicate this to them.

Let us suppose that after completing your education, you want to start a business of your own, but you do not have adequate information or know-how to help you go about it. According to the first magical step in the previous chapter, you need to observe already established and experienced businessmen in your chosen field. Hence, you should develop relationships which will help you closely observe their ways of working. Each experienced businessman is your teacher, from whom you learn the skill and knack of doing business. Gradually, you learn the intricacies that you need to know and become an expert in your field.

Now imagine that you return to thank them and express your appreciation of their business methods. You tell them how much you admire their techniques and how much you have benefited by applying them. Further, you praise them by saying, "You are an excellent and creative business leader." If you praise them genuinely, they will be both pleased and encouraged to excel even further at their work. By showing appreciation, you will not only act as a catalyst for enhancing their performance, but you will also gain their trust more easily. They may even call you again to share more business tips.

In this manner, you can propel others' efficiency to reach new heights. Now let us understand the impact of appreciation through another example.

A college professor was very popular for his unique way of teaching. Once, one of his students expressed his appreciation for the professor's style. "The humor you insert into your lectures makes your sessions really enjoyable and effective. I've listened to many speakers, but few are as talented at using humor to illustrate and inform. You have a real gift for combining the subject with fitting examples, jokes, and anecdotes. This is your special talent." Until then, the professor had not been aware of the importance of this quality. From then on, he made conscious efforts to spice up his sessions with humor, and students welcomed his lectures with even more enthusiasm.

There are many talented people around you; some are good linguists, some are good sportsmen, some are good musicians, some are good teachers, and so on. You should openly admire their qualities. By doing so, you not only change your outlook towards people but your attention will always be drawn towards their best qualities. Therefore, whenever you come into contact with anyone, always think of a reason why you like them: their smile, their smartness, their good behavior, their frankness, their calmness, their good dressing sense, or any other characteristic you notice. Try thinking enthusiastically in this manner and you will discover how well your observational powers develop.

During conversations with different people, if you convey how much you appreciate them and what qualities you like in them, then they too will take an interest in you. Thus, you enhance your social relationships. Your heartfelt compliments can encourage them to raise their own abilities higher. This leads to the development of strong mutual bonds. The tool of appreciation is a magical one, but most people use it too sparingly. They think that by appreciating others, they are underrating themselves. Hence, their conversation focuses instead on finding fault. Without hesitation, they will describe another's weaknesses in detail, which generally leads to argument and a rift in the relationship.

People who understand the importance of human relations follow the Golden Rule of relationships: *Behave with people in the way you want them to behave with you – the real you.* So, following this Golden Rule, never behave with others in a way that you do not want them to behave with you. This is the foremost message of every religion, community, wise sage, and saint. Follow this rule and see each one of your relationships transformed miraculously. Whenever you find anyone worthy of praise, never lose an opportunity to praise them generously.

Furthermore, instead of finding fault or criticizing others, be a 'CritiGuide' and when necessary provide guidance for others' improvement. Refrain from pointing out anybody's mistakes bluntly. For example, if one day at home you find there is too much salt in your food or too little sugar in your tea, does it really matter if you do not point out such faults immediately? Anyway, the one who served you will most probably have the same food or tea and realize it on their own. Therefore, discover and appreciate the good aspects of the food you are served instead, and see how it improves in the future. Pay careful attention to what you say to others. Criticism or praise once uttered, always remains in the other person's memory. It is treated as evidence of whether you are being a good or a bad person in their eyes.

Become convinced that it is a mistake to believe you can change people by criticizing them. Criticism can never improve anyone;

in fact it will make things worse, not least if we point out flaws or blame someone in front of others. We should realize that criticism and cynicism only worsen others' habits and lead them towards misfortune. In addition, we are performing bad karma ourselves, which will return to us with bitter fruit. Even if criticism does result in a temporary improvement in someone's ways, it paves the way to hell in the future. Consider the following examples:

- We know Adolf Hitler received criticism from his childhood. When he grew up, he gave back to the world what he had received by causing unthinkable destruction.
- The daughter-in-law who was always criticized by her mother-in-law usually gives the same treatment to her own daughter-in-law.
- The teacher who was taught as a student with the language of the cane will employ the same methods with his own students.
- A child who is strictly disciplined by his father will raise his kids in the same way.

Hence, you must end this vicious cycle of criticism, which otherwise goes on and on.

> Once a dog bit the manager of a company on his way to work. The manager reached his office late, which caused his boss to reproach him. The manager flushed out his anger at his deputy, who in turn yelled at his subordinate, who passed it on to his clerk. The clerk got annoyed with his assistant for a minor clerical error. The assistant then blasted the office boy for misfiling a document. When the office boy returned home, he got angry when his mother asked why he'd forgotten to collect their groceries. The mother duly vented her annoyance at her youngest son for demanding his supper. The little boy then ran out of the house, picked up a stone and hit the dog who had bitten the company manager. The infuriated dog started searching for another victim. This is how the vicious cycle of anger has no end.

In this world, we each consider ourselves to be important and we do not expect or welcome criticism. Instead we do always welcome appreciation. If you really want to live a peaceful life, then appreciate others sincerely and imbibe their good qualities yourself.

All around you, including your family and other relatives, there are many talented people. If you like something about someone, do tell that person right away. Someone may have a good voice, they may be a good sportsperson, they may write good poems, they may dance well or cook well. Someone may have beautiful handwriting, some may complete every job on time, speak with confidence, donate generously, or always carry a lovely smile. You must show appreciation for all good qualities. Your attention must always be on their positive characteristics. Tell them what you admire in them and they will feel good. Everybody in this world wants appreciation and work hard to earn such words. Therefore, make it a point to praise them.

> Once, a speaker was invited by a company to deliver a speech. On his way to the hall, he saw a notice-board on which something was written in beautiful handwriting. Reading it, he thought, "Whoever has written this has an excellent talent." On enquiring, he found that it was written by the company watchman. After his speech, he made a point of speaking to the watchman and told him, "Your writing is exquisite, with great attention to detail. I really admire you for it." The watchman was elated; he rarely received so much regard, and no one had ever praised his handwriting. He was so happy, he could hardly sleep that night. For the first time in his life, someone had lauded him, and in a loving way. You too can learn to notice and acknowledge the good qualities in others.

Along with this virtue, you should also learn the art of forgiving. If you can forgive yourself, you can also forgive others. Thinking repeatedly of someone who has offended you means that you continue to seethe within. Such thoughts as, "Why did he do that to me… is that the way to behave?" haunt you all day. Therefore, you should learn to forgive. Whatever was done, it was done according to that person's level of understanding. What is your own level of understanding? Is it not higher? You are at a higher level of consciousness, therefore you should forgive. Forgiveness helps both of you to off-load the burden and pain of anguish and resentment.

Learn to CritiGuide

If someone is doing something wrong it is essential, nevertheless, to point out their mistake; without correction they may not improve. But what is the best way to do this? You have to learn to *CritiGuide.* CritiGuidance is a method of criticizing a person by drawing attention to their mistake while also providing corrective guidance. If a student makes some errors in a diagram, the tutor instead of criticizing can say, "There are some minor errors, but you have done a good job and it can easily be improved, in this way…" Thus, along with giving appreciation, you have also pointed out and explained mistakes.

Imagine you have delegated a task to a subordinate but he has not been able to do it very well. You can tell him, "Don't worry. Your work is very efficient and I'm sure you will complete this job just fine. I faced similar challenges when I started, so I'm confident you will easily steer through these issues." You would love to experience the effect of such words. Stay away from criticism and develop the habit of appreciating and encouraging.

Criticism is like an itch. It increases by scratching. When we scratch a wound to soothe the itching, we feel relief and a kind of pleasure. But rapidly the scratching further aggravates the itching, and the condition of the wound becomes worse. People who are always critical of those around them make this scratching habit a part of their life. They not only spoil others' lives but their own life as well.

By criticizing others, an individual feels superior. This is an illusion of greatness that does not benefit the individual in any way. If someone slips on a banana peel and falls, people laugh. They think they are smarter and this makes them feel happy. But superiority is not proved by another person falling down. Therefore, we need to stop concocting such venom, because the world is busy enough criticizing all the time. Without any endeavor, merely by criticizing, we feel we are better than others. We must stop this vicious cycle and free ourselves from the illusion that laughing at and disparaging others implies our superiority.

> Once, a king went to the forest to hunt with his assistant. They had no luck finding prey that day. As dusk fell, they were left with only a wild apple in their hands to eat. The king cut the apple in half and gave one half to his faithful assistant. The assistant quickly ate it and asked for more. Surprised, the king gave him half of the remaining apple and the assistant quickly gulped it down as well. Now the king decided it was time to take a bite himself, but immediately spat out the apple because it was sour. With curiosity, the king asked his assistant how he could eat such sour fruit. The man replied, "Your Majesty, for years I have been given the best of food under your roof, how could I complain if just once I receive a sour apple?"

This story conveys the foolishness of complaining about one or two bitter experiences with those who have always been good to us. Does it make sense to put the entire blame on the other person? We can certainly tolerate occasional unpleasant incidents by remembering the goodness and security of the relationship we have had with them. We can forgive them and give them our love. Through such responses, we set an example for bringing about harmony in relations.

Welcome your critics

There is another facet of criticism to be understood. You have become aware of the truth about criticism, and the need to stop criticizing others. However, if you meet a critic who starts counting all your faults, do not argue with them. Listen to them carefully with patience, because by pointing out your shortcomings they are helping you to become better.

Once, there was an artist who completed a painting and showed it to his painter friend. But this friend, who was jealous of him, pointed out many flaws. The artist did not feel offended or discouraged.

Instead, he corrected all the flaws identified by his friend and showed the painting to him once more. His friend found yet more flaws, and so the artist amended his painting again. He did not get upset, because he felt his proficiency was increasing each time in this process. He continued to seek his friend's opinion and make improvements until no more faults could be found. As a result, he developed into a wonderfully skillful artist, and within a few years became world renowned. Unfortunately, his artist friend remained in his same humble condition. Had he focused on improving his own skills, instead of only pointing out faults of others, he too might have become a world famous painter.

If you can dare to take criticism, and welcome your critics, then you will be helping yourself. Criticism is beneficial; it is feedback for free. So take full advantage by making proper use of it. But before criticizing anyone else, it is important to think through the following questions and only then decide whether to critiguide an individual or not:

1) Is it necessary to criticize?

Suppose an acquaintance tells you the moon is 400,000 km away from Earth, and you know the exact distance is 402,336 km. Is it necessary to correct him harshly, criticize him for his inaccuracy, and spoil a relationship over this point? Of course not. You can simply agree because the detail is of little importance to you, or to the moon.

In contrast, if you find a person playing with a loaded revolver, it is entirely justifiable to remonstrate with that person. Immediate action and clear criticism is required to gain attention. Without this, if the individual is unaware that the gun is loaded, he may harm himself or others.

2) Before you criticize anyone, ascertain if you are correct.

In a particular Hindi movie, the actor Mehmood is depicted as a man ridiculed by others for the dark color of his skin. The other characters consider themselves to be superior as they are lighter skinned. Then Mehmood sings the song: *'So what if I am black, I am a man with a beautiful and loving heart...*' and this puts a stop to their criticism. Whether black or white is superior – it all depends on the eye of the beholder. We admire the color black when a little black mole on a white complexion is seen as a sign of beauty. In contrast, even a small white spot on a black complexion looks like a skin disease. If seen from this perspective, it is as false to condemn a black complexion as it is to admire a white complexion. Hence, look from all possible angles to determine if you are correct before criticizing anyone for anything.

3) Is it possible to critiguide someone without saying anything? Is it possible to convey everything without saying a word?

A mother was inspecting her son's report card. She spoke as she read it out loud: "You scored 55 percent in Hindi, that's good. In English, you got 60 percent, which is also good. You have done very well in Mathematics with 80 percent. You scored 65 percent in Science, 60 percent in History and 72 percent in Civics, which are all good too." The child, in fact, had received only 35 per cent in Geography, but the mother made no comment upon this, silently signed the report card, and gave her son a smile. As her son left the room, the lady's friend who was also present, said: "You appreciated your son for all the subjects where he scored well, but you didn't say anything about Geography in which he scored poorly!" At this, the mother replied, "Last time, he scored badly in math but I didn't comment on it. Because of that, he scored 80 percent this time." As his mother had made no mention of his Geography result, the child clearly understood that his mother had not overlooked it, but was disappointed about it. The child would now work on this subject with more attention. This is the art of conveying everything by saying nothing.

Just understand that there are numerous ways to critiguide. If you think through and choose the right method, it will lead that person towards progress; you will also get the intended results. Explore all possible ways and you will excel in the art of critiguiding people.

For example, you can apply the technique that doctors use for their patients. A doctor does not give consultation to a patient at a public place. He will call the patient to his clinic for a consultation and listen to their problems with full attention and concern. He will then gently assure them saying, "There is nothing to worry about; this is a minor problem. You will be absolutely fine within a few days." Such conduct cures almost half of the patient's illness, even without treatment. As necessary, the doctor may also prescribe some bitter medicine in sugar-coated pills, which also works wonders.

In the same fashion, if you have to give some negative feedback to someone, first offer them some sweet but true words. Before you reproach them, first praise them for their good qualities. This will help them digest your reproach as well. If you adopt this method, you will find that people behave well with you and they also work on improving themselves. You will discover that they now actually like you and will support you whenever you need them.

Encouragement Makes A Quick Impact

To master the skill of encouraging your relatives, friends, and colleagues, you need to understand when and why people behave well, and use this information to encourage them. This means they need to know how they can benefit. *People are not interested in hearing you talk about your personal needs; therefore, first tell them how they will benefit from your advice.*

A father tells his son that he should eat nutritious food. He constantly asks him to drink milk and eat vegetables and fruits so that he will grow strong with the right vitamins. But the child never heeds his father. One day, he returns home beaten up by a friend. His father tells him, "See, had you taken my advice about nutritious food, you could have taught your friend a tough lesson." Once the child has realized the benefits of nutritious food, he will start listening to his father's advice. You can apply this technique in many circumstances.

Each person has his own way of encouraging others. The day you understand the importance of encouragement, your relationships will change dramatically. All your friends, relatives, and neighbors will be pleased at your taking this second step. Now all of you together can change the world by taking the third step, which follows.

22

*Transmit only good news
and you will make everyone happy.*

MAGICAL STEP 3: BECOME A GOOD NEWS REPORTER
How to transform the world

The first magical step showed us how we can benefit ourselves. The second step demonstrated how we can benefit the people around us. The third magical step illustrates how we can benefit the entire world.

At the third step, you have to become a GNR – a Good News Reporter.

Every morning, you may read a newspaper or website, or watch a news channel, that presents news from around the world. There will be news of murders, atrocities, abductions, robberies, violence, terrorism, and more. You carry this news in your mind, then talk about it with your friends and colleagues during the day. In turn, you hear about more such events and incidents from them. As a result, you accumulate more and more negative news in your head.

From now on, consider focusing only on news that highlights the good and best of events around the world and in your own society. For example, news of a student who topped university exams, invention of something beneficial, someone who has won a gold medal in sports, a great achievement by someone with a handicap, the risky saving of someone's life, the publishing of a good book, a summer camp for disadvantaged children, a free medical camp for the underprivileged, success in protecting and improving the environment, and so on. If you talk only about good things, you will hear the same from others. This is because you are setting the agenda and others will respond with similar types of news.

Let us understand how the principle of GNR works. Suppose you share a good news story with your friend, and he too shares one with you. Now you will have two good news stories to share with the next person you meet. This person in turn shares other good news with you and also passes on your good news to other people. They in turn continue to spread good news. In this way, a single item of good news multiplies into a wave of positive news that spreads quickly. Now people will always want to receive good news from you because you make them feel lighter and happier. If you are always cheerful and happy and transmit only good news, everyone will seek your company and look forward to hearing entertaining tales, good news, and inspiring stories from you.

By always presenting yourself in this way, you can transform the whole world and make everyone happy. Do not feel concerned about how you can do this alone. You can do it alone. Just remember, if you choose, you can change the entire world and make it a better place. The following is the proof of how this is possible.

You know that a chessboard comprises 64 squares. Take a chessboard and start placing wheat grains on each of the squares. The only rule is that you have to double the number of grains you place as you move from one square to the next. In the first square you place one grain, in the second square two grains, in the third square four grains, in the fourth square eight grains, and so on. Now, the question is, how many grains will you need for the 64th square?

It may be difficult for you to estimate an exact figure. Think of this, perhaps, in terms of volume. Would it require one kg or one sack of wheat? Or would it require the wheat needed to supply a whole city for one day? Would it require the volume of wheat needed to feed a whole nation for a day?

In fact, the volume of wheat needed for the 64th square would make a heap bigger than Mount Everest. This is not only more than the one-day wheat production of one country like India. It is not only more than the one-day wheat production of the world. It adds up to several times the world's wheat production! That is the power of exponential growth.

This example is intended to convey that you can start with the spreading of good news, just like the spreading of wheat grains on the chess board, and the same principles will apply. When you convey good news to your friends, they pass it on to their friends. Suppose you and your friends pass on the good news to four people. Those four people introduce the good news to eight others. In this way, eight, sixteen, thirty-two, sixty-four people... ultimately, the whole world can be reached with your good news and that of others. With the additional power today of cell phones and social media, you have no reason to doubt or be daunted by the prospect of changing the world.

The chart on the next page will erase all your doubts. Read the chart carefully and then decide to become a GNR now.

Sixty-four Squares on a Chessboard and The Secret to Transform the World

Square	Wheat	Comment
1	1 grain	
2	2 grains	
3	4 grains	
4	8 grains	
5	16 grains	
6	32 grains	
7	64 grains	
8	128 grains	
9	256 grains	
10	512 grains	861 grains weigh 50 grams
11	50 grams	1024 grains weigh more than 50 grams
12	100 grams	
13	200 grams	
14	400 grams	
15	800 grams	
16	1.5 kg	1000 grams make 1 kg of wheat

Square	Wheat	Comment
17	3 kg	
18	6 kg	
19	12 kg	
20	24 kg	
21	48 kg	
22	1½ sacks	1 sack of wheat contains approximately 40-50 kg
23	3 sacks	
24	6 sacks	
25	12 sacks	
26	24 sacks	
27	48 sacks	
28	96 sacks	
29	192 sacks	
30	384 sacks	
31	768 sacks of wheat means 2 truckloads of wheat	1 truck can carry approx. 200-300 sacks of wheat
32	4 truckloads	Half the chessboard is covered here
33	8 truckloads	
34	16 truckloads	
35	1 coach	2 truckloads of wheat can be carried by a coach in a goods train

122 / CELEBRATING RELATIONSHIPS

Square	Wheat	Comment
36	2 coaches	
37	4 coaches	
38	8 coaches	
39	16 coaches	Meaning one goods train
40	2 goods trains	
41	4 goods trains	
42	8 goods trains	
43	16 goods trains	
44	32 goods trains	32 goods trains of wheat would be approx. equal to one-day harvest for a city
45	Harvest for 2 cities	
46	4 cities	
47	8 cities	
48	16 cities	
49	32 cities	32 cities = 1 State in a nation like India
50	2 states	
51	4 states	
52	8 states	
53	16 states	
54	32 states	Approx. 32 states = 1 nation like India
55	2 nations	

Square	Wheat	Comment
56	4 nations	
57	8 nations	8 nations like India = 1 Earth
58	2 Earths	
59	!	You can do the remaining calculations
60	! !	
61	! ! !	
62	! ! ! !	
63	! ! ! ! !	
64	! ! ! ! ! !	

CELEBRATING RELATIONSHIPS / 123

Today, thousands of people are reading this book and participating in this family retreat, which means there are already more than 1000 people on the first square of the GNR chess board. Hence, it will not be difficult to spread good news and raise the level of consciousness of the world.

Regarding the chessboard example:

1) The numbers given in each of the 64 boxes are approximate. They have been under-estimated only to avoid any doubts.

2) The UN and the US Census Bureau estimate the population of India to be 1/6th of the world. Therefore, it can be said that the population of the world or this Earth corresponds to approximately six Indias. But to remove any possible doubts, eight Indias have been considered in the calculations.

3) The 57th square contains the wheat production of one Earth. The 58th square contains the wheat of two Earths. Now you can see the astonishing power of this principle.

4) If you still doubt this math, you cannot deny that more than this Earth's wheat would definitely be required to fill the board.

5) Instead of wheat grains, consider each wheat grain as a GNR. Do you now think it would be difficult for GNRs to transform the world?

Come, let us all become GNRs and spread positive and happy thoughts. And to do so:

- Observe the good all around you and enhance your own good qualities.
- Appreciate the good qualities in others and benefit them.
- Resolve to make your Good News Reporting benefit the entire world.

These are the three magical steps to improve relationships. In the next chapter, let us learn the golden method that will help you break the glass walls that have developed between relationships.

Section VI

BREAK DOWN WALLS AND CONNECT WITH PEOPLE, GURU, AND GOD

23

*We must see how a person is right;
not how they are wrong.*

How To Break The Walls Between Relationships-1
Golden Method: Glass Breaking

Are you ready to break the glass walls that have built up between your relationships with others? You have already learnt of several dimensions of relationships so that you can mend all the rifts in your relations. After filling in the cracks, now let's start learning the next step in healing your relationships.

During the initial days of friendship, people experience plenty of enthusiasm, freshness, and love. But as time passes, the friendship can lose its charm. There is a lot of respect towards the friend in the early days of the relationship, but with time, this respect wanes. Likewise, newly married couples share a sweet relationship in the beginning, but after some while, the relationship begins to become a little mechanical. When new people move into the neighborhood, curiosity leads neighbors to have good relations with them initially, but after some time, such warmth begins to evaporate. Does this happen with you too? Give honest thought to this important and multifaceted aspect of relationships.

When someone meets you, what do they feel, and how should they actually feel? Recollect how your parents, friends, spouse, children, relatives, neighbors, brothers, sisters, colleagues at work... feel on meeting you. Do they feel happy on meeting you? Do they wish to share their experiences honestly with you? Are they eager to meet you or do they avoid you? Every person wishes to be popular and to be everyone's favorite. Everybody likes to have good relations with everyone. But does this happen automatically? In fact, it really takes some thought and effort.

In order to have warm relations with all, you need to first understand the factors that cause staleness in relationships. The glass wall that gets created unknowingly between relationships is the main problem. This wall is not visible, but it is there. It makes your life mechanical. All the family members who are part of your everyday life – your brothers, sisters, mother, father, children, wife, and so on – you take for granted, and a glass wall forms quickly in these relationships. Until these walls are annihilated, the earlier warmth in these relationships will not return. And the interesting fact is that you may even hear a slight cracking sound when you break these walls. You will feel it when you make the attempt. Let us understand this with a real life example.

> A man had been carrying his entire family's responsibilities for over 22 years. He had dealt with many hardships for the sake of his parents, siblings, and other relatives. One day, an acquaintance told him, "Dear friend! You have sacrificed your life and pleasures for their happiness. You are indeed a great man." Hearing this, the man was overcome with emotion and started sobbing uncontrollably. The acquaintance was taken aback and asked, "I have just expressed my admiration for your deeds, why are you crying?' The man controlled his sobs and replied, "I have been desperately waiting to hear those words for the past 22 years! I wanted to hear someone from my family say that I had endured so many difficulties for them. It is unfortunate, but I have never heard those words until now. You are the first person who has valued me and understood my feelings. I was overwhelmed by your words. At least there is one person who appreciates all the sacrifices I have made." Saying so, tears started rolling down his face again.

Every individual desires his acts and sacrifices to be recognized and appreciated. If you honestly question whether it is the same with you, the answer would be 'yes'. And just as we want to be lauded ourselves, others too are eager to receive their share of praise; but the fact is they never hear it. We are very stingy when it comes to appreciating each other. As a result, an invisible wall of glass gets erected between us. When we sincerely praise someone, the glass wall breaks. From the example above, you can understand how to break the glass wall and how easy it is.

How do we talk to people when we meet them? What do we tell them and what actually should we speak with them about? Do we end up talking only about ourselves or do we also enquire about them? Very often, we are unable to sublimate our ego while talking. To boast about ourselves is our biggest weakness. This is the reason why we fail to establish close relations with our own family members. We find it extremely hard to destroy the glass walls. Our ego does not permit us to bend down, it does not let us speak even a few loving words to others. We must break this ego and only then will we succeed in shattering the glass walls in our relationships.

To begin with, appreciate and praise the virtues, work, and sacrifices of your family members. Often, you may want to express your appreciation for them, but some thoughts hold you back, such as, "What can I say when they are only performing their duty?" In fact, your family members want to hear a few words of appreciation in recognition of their actions time and again. Although their errors are also visible to you, remember you should first praise their positive side. It is possible that you too commit mistakes, in which case, accept them and admit them to your family members.

To break glass walls, you can remember a simple formula:

G: Gratitude. Express your heartfelt gratitude for everything that person has done.

L: Listen attentively and fully to what the person wants to say.

A: Appreciate with sincerity all the wonderful qualities or skills that person has, which has impacted your life as well as those of others.

S: Say, "I am sorry" or "I love you" from the depth of your heart, along with the reasons for it.

S: Sweet gesture - which could be a hug, a flower, a greeting card, chocolates, or any other little gift that the person is fond of.

Some real life examples are presented below that will help you understand how you can bring down the glass walls in your relationships.

Example 1: Father and daughter

A girl got into a big argument with her father just before she left town on some official business. She spent the following day completely engrossed in her work, but in the evening she remembered the quarrel of the previous day. She reflected on the entire situation and was filled with remorse and regret. So she immediately rang up her father and said, "Papa, I love you." Her father was astonished. He couldn't understand what had suddenly happened to his daughter. With concern, he asked, "What has happened, child?' She replied, "Papa, I am truly sorry for my behavior. I do respect you and love you with all my heart." You may imagine her father's reaction. His heart melted. He took a deep breath and said, "Child, come home quickly, I am waiting for you." The glass wall that had crept up due to disagreements and conflicts was shattered in a moment when his daughter said, "I love you." Children never express their love for their parents; they assume they know that they love them. Despite this, parents always wish to hear their children's feelings in words.

Example 2: Mother and son

There was a 16-year-old boy who was always tense because he and his mother quarreled over petty things every day. On his birthday, he went out with his friends and learnt from someone about breaking glass walls. He immediately understood the secret of how to improve his relationship with his mother. So, he called his mother and said, "Mom, today I realized all that you have done for me and how many troubles you have gone through. I want to give you a million thanks." On hearing these words of gratitude from her son, the mother was filled with emotion and burst out crying.

The boy could not hold back his tears either. When he hung up the phone, his friends asked him why he was crying. Engulfed in a sense of love, he said, "These are the tears of my mother's happiness." Imagine how he would have been received by his mother when he returned home!

Example 3: Father and son

There was a boy who was hot tempered and never heeded his mother's words. His mother was distressed by this and was always worried about him. However, as he became older, the boy began to become aware of his bad habits. He started making attempts to mend his ways. Gradually, after understanding the concept of breaking glass walls, he started to work on bringing harmony into the family. This made his mother very happy. However, the boy's father was of a very quiet and serious nature, and never talked openly with his son. Because of this, a glass wall had formed between the two. They were uncomfortable in each other's presence. The one wish the boy had was to hug his father at least once in his life. And at the age of eighteen, he finally hugged his father and realized how deprived he had felt of this simple joy! The father was surprised but also very happy at this expression of love from his son.

Example 4: Two brothers

A student shared an experience with his teacher in the classroom. He told her that once he had got into a fight with someone and had thrashed that person black and blue. After this incident, they had not spoken to each other for almost seven years. One day, after learning about the method of breaking glass walls, he realized his mistake and tried to apply the principle. He told his victim, "I committed a bad mistake. I shouldn't have treated you that way. Please try to forget it. I am ashamed of what I did." The teacher was very impressed with this story and decided to share it with another class. When she told the student's story, the entire class went quiet. Then, one boy suddenly got up and broke the silence. He said, "Mam, that boy is my elder brother. We had a fight, and for seven years we didn't speak to each other. But now we live in love and harmony together."

For seven years they had been bereft of each other's love! Are you also bereft of love in some relationships in your life? Take a lesson from these examples and quickly take appropriate action.

You can hear a sound when glass walls break. The sound could be from sobs, laughter, or celebrations of joy. Do you wish to hear this sound of shattering glass again and again? The next chapter will show you how.

24

*Those who want healthy relations
must eliminate the factors that harm relationships.*

HOW TO BREAK THE WALLS BETWEEN RELATIONSHIPS-2

Golden Method: Glass Breaking

The number of people involved in a person's life can almost double once they enter wedlock. It then becomes a duty to try to maintain these relationships. The following real life examples will help you break the glass walls that are often present in various relationships before and after marriage.

Example 1: Husband and wife

A man married for fifteen years was very appreciative of his wife's contribution towards his life and his entire family's wellbeing and growth. However, engulfed in work, he had never been able to spend quality time with his wife, and many years slipped by in this way. Though living an apparently happily married life, a glass wall had crept up between them. This dried up the stream of love in their hearts, and as a result, their relationship had fallen into mechanical ways. The man decided he should try to overcome this problem in their relationship. But several days passed without his feeling able to freely express what he really wanted to say. When he learnt about glass walls, he understood why there was a barrenness in his life despite having everything. With no further delay, he immediately said to his wife, "Whatever I am today, whatever success I have achieved, it is only because of you. You have made a huge contribution to the well-being and happiness of our family. Please accept my heartfelt gratitude for all you have done over these years." These words filled her with tremendous joy, and she felt satisfied that all the sacrifices she had made for the family had ultimately been purposeful and fruitful.

Example 2: Father-in-law and son-in-law

Once, a young man attending a self-development workshop confessed to the bad behavior that afflicted him, which nearly ruined his life. He said he was a very eccentric and irritable person who simply could not resist the temptation of troubling others. He had the habit of drinking excessively every night and on reaching home being abusive to his father-in-law over the phone. Consequently, his wife had left him and gone to stay at her parents' place. The man was tired of his bad habits and wanted to get rid of them. After understanding the concept of how to break glass walls, he decided to apply this to his father-in-law in an attempt to mend their relationship. Previously, he would just wait for night to fall so that he could ring up his in-laws to vent his fury. But that day he felt a little scared to call them, wondering how he should begin, what he should say, and how he should break the glass wall.

His in-laws often avoided answering his calls because of his spiteful behavior. So he decided to call from a public booth. When his father-in-law answered, he rushed to say, "I am now a completely changed man. I want to apologize for what I have done. Please believe me, I am not the same anymore. I have undergone a radical transformation. Please allow me to talk to my wife." At first, his father-in-law would not believe him, so he relentlessly continued his efforts to convince him. At last, his in-laws were persuaded. His marriage had deteriorated to the extent that divorce was imminent. But this new understanding prevented this misfortune and they got back together.

This real life example is a testimony of how a single phone call can bring about an incredible change in one's life. His transformation inspired many people. They felt that if he can change, so can they! When transformation takes place from within, the individual himself is not aware of how he becomes instrumental in the betterment of many lives.

Example 3: Stepmother and son

A boy lived with his father and step-mother. He loathed his stepmother. Many years before, she had uttered some harsh words, which had hurt him deeply. From then on, their relationship had turned bitter and he maintained a distance from her. Over time, the rift between them widened to the extent that he even stopped calling her 'mother'. However, understanding imparted through the glass breaking technique triggered a major change in his thinking. He started making efforts to rekindle life and love in the relationship. As a result, his disposition softened, and one day he felt able to address her as 'mother'. Just imagine how this lady would have felt on suddenly hearing this from her son who had refused to accept her or address her as his mother for so many years. An ocean of love erupted in her heart.

Example 4: Mother-in-law and daughter-in-law

A lady was having a tough time with her mother-in-law, who would frequently become angry with her and spit out venomous comments. The poor daughter-in-law had become very unhappy and did not know how to change her mother-in-law's attitude towards her. When she learnt about glass breaking, she resolved: "Today, I shall break the wall that exists between us." She went home and sat directly on her mother-in-law's lap. She then declared in a determined voice, "Until and unless you accept me as your daughter, I will not move an inch. You have to call me your daughter and become my mother, only then will I get up from your lap, otherwise I will continue to sit just like this." This shook up her mother-in-law, whose heart then melted like butter. They hugged each other and cried in happiness together.

Even a small action can transform your life and repair all kinds of ruptures in your relationships. Do not assume that you always need to seek an apology. For glass breaking, you can also praise the virtues of others and the good things they have done for you; or give them gifts in return for their love and support.

Example 5: Husband, wife, and profession

A man had been married for over twenty years. His wife was a lawyer by profession, and for the last fifteen years had been successfully juggling her family life and her profession. However, the husband never considered the commendable job his wife was doing in balancing work with the management of their home. He would think, "Why should I thank her? It is her duty." But when his perspective expanded, his heart was filled with gratitude. He realized that the only person responsible for his being relaxed and free from worry was his wife. She had been both efficiently conducting her work and fulfilling all her family responsibilities like caring for the children, getting them ready for school, bringing them home, cooking for everyone, and other chores. For the first time, he felt that he should be infinitely grateful to her. With this thought, he broke the glass wall between them and their relationship was filled again with love.

You can apply the same in your family. Every member of your family is waiting to hear some loving words from you. Be it your brother, your sister, your mother, your father, your spouse, your daughter-in-law, or your in-laws. Everyone wants to hear you say, "I like you; I love you." They want to hear your acknowledgement of the good things they have done for you. Therefore, always express your gratefulness for their good deeds and special qualities. And if you have committed any mistakes, sincerely apologize for them, as this is also a method of glass breaking.

With time, barriers do develop in some relationships. These might be subtle in nature to begin with, but they grow into thick walls over time. You have to regularly make small, or perhaps large, attempts to break these walls. If you come across an acquaintance while walking along a street, give him a smile. This too is glass breaking. Even wishing "Good Morning" to the liftman or greeting the postman with a smile is an act of glass breaking. You have to take the initiative because it is you who have read this book. You should not think that someone from your family or friends should begin glass breaking, and then you will follow. You need to take the first step.

Remember also to look into the eyes of the person while breaking the wall. You will eventually notice a sparkle in their eyes, which indicates the wall breaking. If you do not see any sparkle, it means the wall has yet to completely break. In such cases, you have to take a step further. You can take the other person's hand in yours. Is this possible for you? Can you hug your father? Can you hug your brother and with what intensity? A daughter can hug her mother, a daughter-in-law can sit on her mother-in-law's lap. Can a son-in-law hug his mother-in-law? Yes, he can. But, whatever is to be done, it must be done this very day. You may think of doing it tomorrow, but nothing happens tomorrow. Whatever can happen will happen only today, now, at this moment.

It is you who have to begin with the glass breaking. And you have to start with your family. Every reader is sincerely requested to make this attempt. With whomever you want to break the glass, do so right NOW. You only have to look toward the love in that person, not their faults. You can carry out the glass breaking with whoever you wish and in any way that you wish, even by phone, email or text message, but do so completely. What happens following the glass breaking will be the golden period of your life. You will remember the moment as long as you live.

Since glass walls are invisible, it never occurs to us to demolish them. These walls are formed in relationships at home as well as between friends, customers, and colleagues. The examples given in the next chapter will throw more light on this.

25

*When we repent, we renew ourself
and begin to lead a pure life again.*

How To Break The Walls Between Relationships-3

Golden Method: Glass Breaking

Do you know any relationships in which there are no glass walls? These glass walls are everywhere. This is because the glass walls are a creation of the mind. The human mind is expert at making assumptions. Each assumption made in ignorance and unawareness creates a glass wall of misunderstanding. The moment you make an assumption about anyone should make you alert. You should think, "Since I don't have complete information, could it be that the assumption I am making is simply wrong?" Your alertness toward making assumptions will slow down the formation of the wall. Below are some real life examples to help you break glass walls in every relationship.

Example 1: The family

A boy lost his father during his childhood. His mother was a resilient lady. She had taken the entire responsibility of the household on her shoulders and ensured that she gave her children the love of both parents. The boy had great respect for his mother, but was hesitant to express his feelings and hence had never told her what he felt for her. Upon learning the technique of glass breaking, he expressed his love and respect for her in these words: "Our family is strong and we are all bonded by love. I realize this has been possible only due to you and it makes me so happy." On hearing these words, her eyes glistened with tears and she hugged her son.

This joy can be experienced at any time, but we habitually think, "What's the hurry? I can do it tomorrow. I love my family and I am concerned for the well-being of each of them, so what is the need to say it now in words?" But it is very important that love be expressed in words and actions. If you are able to do the glass breaking today, it's possible for you to do it in the future as well. It is essential to do glass breaking in the family every two to three months. And every time, rejoice in the joy that follows.

Example 2: Two friends

There were two friends. One of them often travelled abroad on work. He never brought back gifts for his friend, but he always made sure to buy a gift for his friend's son. What warm emotions would be created in the father's mind by his friend's actions! What a simple way to arouse good feelings in others. It is a wonderful feeling to know that you are remembered by your loved ones. When you travel somewhere, and bring back small gifts for your family's or friend's children, they will remember you always because you have subtly broken the glass wall with them. You expressed love for the one they love dearly. This is a significant way to enhance and strengthen relations.

Example 3: Glass breaking on the phone

There was a lawyer who had a bad relationship with his brother. They clashed endlessly over almost anything. But one day, the lawyer decided that their feud was enough, and he must break the wall separating them. He rang up his brother but immediately forgot he had called for glass breaking and they began fighting as usual. After some time, he remembered why he had phoned. He told his brother, "I actually called you to apologize. I have made many blunders with you in the past. Please forget and ignore them, and please forgive me." His brother was touched and let bygones be bygones. The two brothers talked lovingly for half an hour more. How easy it became after gaining understanding!

Example 4: Birthday greetings to customers

There was a gentleman who always remembered the birthdays and anniversaries of all his relatives, friends, and acquaintances. He would never forget to send greeting cards and flowers to all of them on their special days. When he was asked to share his experiences, he said, "Very often, people do not even remember their own birthdays. On receiving my greeting, that person and their family get a reminder, and then they celebrate the special occasion."

Once, he sent a birthday greeting to an acquaintance, but on that day the family was engaged in major clashes. As soon as the greeting card arrived, however, everyone remembered the birthday and their fighting stopped. In this way, the greetings sent by the gentleman became a wonderful medium to end conflict and bring joy back to a family.

Do we remember the birthdays of others? Do we remember the birthdays of our nearest and dearest? Wishing happiness to those close to us on their birthdays is also a subtle way of glass breaking.

Example 5: Manager and his family

A business manager had a nasty argument with his wife and ended up abusing her with violence. She left him and went to stay with her parents along with her child. After a month, the man managed to pacify his wife and she and the child returned. But his in-laws remained angry with him after the incident and wouldn't allow him in their house. After learning about glass breaking, he called them up, but the family were not willing to speak to him. So, he drove to their house, but was confronted by his angry brother-in-law at the entrance itself. The man immediately touched his brother-in-law's feet, apologized profusely, and promised never to mistreat his sister again. He then pleaded that he be allowed to speak to his mother-in-law to apologize. The brother-in-law was stunned by his changed behavior and eventually allowed him inside. The man then took his mother-in-law's hand, bent his knee and said, "I have committed a grave sin by ill-treating my wife, and I have insulted you. I know you are very angry with me, and you are right to have banished me from your house. But today, I realize my dreadful mistake. I am ashamed of what I have done. I swear that I will never hurt you or your daughter again. Please treat me as your son, and let go of the anger and hatred in your heart." After such glass breaking, the wall did break, and today they have very good relations with each other.

In a similar manner, a family can perform glass breaking collectively with their relatives. It is possible that your relatives will experience even more happiness than you because no one may have done such a thing with them before. If you have understood the importance of glass breaking, you will bring it into action. When you break the glass with anyone, they will remember you throughout their life and will thank you forever.

By now, you will have understood that beyond your family you can also break the glass with friends, neighbors, associates, and anyone else. Decide today who the people are with whom you want to break down glass walls. Invite them or meet them on the pretext of festivals or anniversaries or birthdays, and thank them for being there and show your appreciation for them. Listen to what they have to say. Then, if you have committed any mistakes with them, sincerely seek their forgiveness. This is glass breaking, this is how you break the walls between relationships.

If every society adopts this technique, a wave of love and peace will engulf every country. All kinds of violence and riots will come to an end. The glass walls between religions give rise to violence and the glass walls between nations give rise to wars. Break them today, and listen to the walls falling apart. Then watch the whole world become one.

26

*Those who can forgive themselves
can also forgive others.*

LEARN THE ART OF FORGIVING AND FORGETTING
Ability to forgive

If you want to bring love and peace into your life, you must increase your ability to forgive. Those who forgive are easily forgiven.

Everyone deserves to be forgiven because everyone makes mistakes. Everyone makes mistakes because of: lack of information, inability to read other's thoughts, and occasional carelessness.

It may be that you are able to forgive someone for small incidents but not major ones. To enable you to forgive people for all their mistakes, you need to learn the art of forgiving in the right way. When you practice forgiveness for small incidents, you can then succeed in forgiving for bigger incidents as well. Do not jump directly to big incidents.

When you are unable to forgive someone for big mistakes, it means that you want to punish them; or you want to punish yourself by thinking about the mistakes again and again. Therefore, first assess if you are able to forgive other people at all – at least for minor transgressions. Do you feel the need to forgive? Ask yourself if you have developed the higher understanding of forgiveness. Higher understanding tells us that the same Consciousness pervades each one of us. So do we actually need to forgive 'others'? Are there any 'others' to forgive? By obtaining answers to all these questions, you must increase your level of consciousness at every step.

It's okay if you cannot forgive major mistakes at present. But your mental framework needs to enable you to view every incident from a higher viewpoint. To forgive does not mean that you say nothing about an incident. It is important that errors are pointed out so that mistakes are not repeated. This can be done by explaining errors to the person and conveying to them that they fail to consider certain points while carrying out a particular task, which leads to errors. You can also tell them in good words to reflect on what you have told them and to respond accordingly in similar situations in the future. Thus, while forgiving, you can also mediate change in behavior through such communication.

While we learn to forgive, we must also learn to ask for forgiveness from others for our own mistakes. Do not think that if someone is not able to forgive you now, then they will never be able to do so. If someone cannot forgive you now, then you must consider their 'no' as meaning 'not now'. When the other person says, "I cannot forgive you," you can ask them for forgiveness again after some time has elapsed. By doing so, it is quite possible that due to the healing effect of time and your correct way of seeking forgiveness, they may forgive you. This will be beneficial for them too; you should also seek forgiveness so that the other person can escape from the clutches of hatred. Your mindset behind asking for forgiveness should be one of love.

It may happen that after forgiving or seeking forgiveness, thoughts of hostility begin to return after some time. At such times, try to remember what it is that you have forgotten. With what understanding had you forgiven? What have you forgotten that has enabled negative thoughts to return? If you can recall the insight that you previously had, then you can easily come out of your hatred.

Forgiving and being forgiven, both yield happiness. You cannot escape happiness in both these situations. You will feel good when someone forgives you and you will also feel good when you forgive someone. A happy person is always forgiving.

In situations where you are unable to forgive, ask yourself, "Who has committed this mistake? What is my relationship with them? Who needs to forgive? And who is feeling bad?" If the other person has committed a mistake, then is it due to lack of understanding or information? Under what assumptions were they operating? Contemplate these questions honestly. In this way, the incident and your act of forgiveness will result in your further progress in life. They will lead you to self-enquiry and self-observation. Forgiveness will remind you of your higher self and elevate you.

As the first step in the process of forgiving, you should understand that by forgiving, you will be the first to be liberated from negative feelings. By being forgiven, the other person may or may not feel liberated, but by giving forgiveness you are definitely liberated.

If you do not forgive, negative thoughts will continue to churn inside you. You will always be seeking a chance to point out the other person's mistake, to put them down, and make them pay. Your focus will unnecessarily be on lower thoughts. When you meet people with whom you are angry, your focus will not be on the present, but caught up in memories of the past.

It is lack of forgiveness that will prevent you from staying in the present. Since the present is the only truth, learn to forgive and stay in the present. Assess yourself in every incident, elevate your understanding, forgive others, and free yourself.

Negative incidents do occur in life. We feel miserable and sad by constantly remembering them, and allowing feelings of guilt and hatred to grow in our minds. It is of no use recollecting such incidents, they only make us sick.

Feelings of malice, hatred, and envy hidden inside us may pop up according to the situation. For example, a relative who insulted you in your childhood may still make you feel bad whenever you cross paths. He may not even remember the incident, but you still recollect it and feelings of hatred bubble up each time you meet. What you need to do is forget the incident and forgive him. Otherwise, you will continue to get upset and your mind will never be free from pain.

Similarly, any incident that reminds you of a mistake you made in the past can arouse feelings of guilt and self-hate in your mind. It is not wrong to remember such incidents, but the arousal of guilt and hatred is painful and unnecessary. Recollecting the same incidents over and over only makes you miserable and sad. It is unnecessary to lead your life carrying such a burden in your head.

Some people say that they neither hate anyone nor do they harbor any guilt feelings. But then, from where does the hatred appear when it does arise? It can only be that the hatred is present inside. We have to treat ourselves for such hatred, and not the other person. It is we who need the medicine and not others.

Seeing a person, different feelings awaken in different people. Like, some feel angry, some fear, some love, some happiness, some sympathy, some hatred, some jealousy, and some envy. How can one person create such a variety of feelings in all these different people? This only means that those particular feelings were already present in those people, which were only brought to the surface on seeing that person. If we feel hatred for someone, it indicates that hatred is already present inside us and that person only acts as a trigger for the hatred to express. But we believe that this person is somehow in the wrong and that their behavior needs to change. We believe that if only they could be changed then we would be happy. But this is an illusion. If we wish to achieve change then it has to come from within ourselves. We need to understand that: "I do not need to improve any other person, I need to improve myself. I do not have to change the world, I have to change myself." Harboring negative feelings in our minds invites a lot of physical and mental ills. The sooner we are convinced that change needs to come from ourselves, the earlier we will be free from hatred and guilt.

We run away from things that we do not like to see or hear. Some people cannot stand to see untidiness, filth, poverty, or disease. Some cannot bear the sound of rock music, noisy voices, vehicle horns, or barking dogs. Furthermore, some cannot listen to criticism, even of their favorite politician, actor, or singer. In this way, we accept only one aspect of life. We accept the good things and reject and run away from the bad. We sway between the game of acceptance and non-acceptance, of joy and sorrow. This struggle continues throughout life.

The truth is that it is only because of sorrow that joy has value. It is only due to our enemies that friends have value. We value honest people because dishonest ones exist too. If sorrow was removed from life then joy would vanish too. Hence, learn to see both sides of the coin, so that it becomes easy to forgive others.

How to increase the capacity for forgiveness

The procedure of forgiveness is described briefly below. You can carry out the following experiments by sitting in a relaxed position on a chair for 10–15 minutes in solitude, or you can practice lying down.

In childhood, due to an inability to distinguish between right and wrong, a person may harbor hatred for his own parents. Memories of childhood may haunt such a person even after growing up. Therefore, in this experiment, first bring your parents mentally to view in front of your eyes. Perhaps they rebuked or hit you in your childhood. Perhaps they had loved your brother or sister more than you. Perhaps they prevented you from going somewhere you really wanted to go or from associating with friends, or they said negative things about your friends, for which you still feel anger towards them. Now recollect those incidents, one by one, before your eyes. Understand that whatever your parents did was appropriate to their level of understanding, fear, or ignorance at that time. Consider it in this way and forgive them.

Whatever a person does, it is done according to the level of understanding or information available to them at the time. Therefore, understand that whatever happened was according to such understanding, which is not the same today. Forgive others in accordance with your present understanding. Your understanding is different today. View past incidents with today's understanding and you will not consider them as bad as they had seemed. In your mind, convey these thought to your parents: *"I love you, I forgive you. Please forgive me too."*

At times, your siblings may have distressed you. They have complained about you, they have ignored you, they have insulted you, or they have treated you in a way you felt you did not deserve. Recall such incidents mentally, one after the other, in front of your eyes. Everything that your siblings did to you was according to their level of understanding at that point of time; in other respects, they are still your well-wishers.

Whatever and whenever someone does something that is hurtful, it is according to the governing influences at that time, such as fear, ignorance, or lack of higher consciousness. When you look at the mistakes committed by your siblings with this understanding, your ability to forgive will increase. Now forgive your siblings for everything they did in the past. Tell them in your mind, *"I love you, I forgive you, and you too please forgive me. This is for the well-being of all. Now I am free from hatred; and I am liberating you as well."*

In this way, the sacred water of forgiveness will cleanse away all your feelings of hatred. People you hated will also become free from the clutches of your resentment. You can use this technique to forgive every relative, friend or associate with whom it is needed – be it grandparents, uncles, aunts, doctors, teachers, police, neighbors, boss, etc. Whether or not others are liberated from hatred, you will definitely be liberated.

When you harbor loathing towards someone in your mind, then first you harm yourself. After this experiment, ask yourself whether you succeeded in forgiving yourself and others. Forgiving others is not a favor you do to them, but to yourself. So do yourself a favor by forgiving others and yourself.

Prepare a list of those you want to forgive. If you cannot forgive everyone at the same time, then forgive one by one, every day, following the technique described above.

27

*See virtues in everyone
because the virtue you focus on grows inside you as well.*

CONNECTION BETWEEN RELATIONS AND THOUGHTS
Rule of life and progress in relationships

A king sat at the window of his palace every morning and watched a wood-cutter setting out for his work. The wood-cutter passed by the palace every day on his way to cut wood in the forest. He would set out very early each morning, even in the biting cold. Seeing this, the king felt both sadness and sympathy for this hard-working man.

In the evening, the king would watch the wood-cutter pass by once more as he returned from the forest. But each time that he watched him return, he experienced feelings of disgust and hatred for this man. This pattern became part of the king's daily routine.

The king was confused by this contradiction in his thoughts. After reflection, he called his wise minister and asked him what might be the reason for this paradox. The minister asked for two days, after which he would definitely provide the king with an answer that solved this mystery.

Before you continue to read this story, think about what has been conveyed so far. Why does the king have conflicting thoughts – sympathy in the morning and hatred in the evening – about the same person? This is the secret you have to learn. If you once understand this story and apply its lessons in your life, then you won't need to be reminded again of the significance of thoughts.

To continue with the tale, the minister went to the wood-cutter's house disguised as a simple traveler. He enquired after the wood-cutter's welfare and then asked him about his work. The wood-cutter replied that he was doing okay and his work made him just enough money to survive. The minister found nothing out of the ordinary with the man. But as they continued talking, the minister noticed a closed room at the back of the house. With curiosity, he asked the man what was inside the room. The wood-cutter replied that he was collecting sandalwood in the room, and that he had a special purpose in mind. On further probing, he revealed that he was collecting the sandalwood to be used for the grand funeral pyre that would be needed once the king died. At such a time, he believed he would be able to ask for twice or three times its normal value.

After listening to the wood-cutter, the minister now understood why the king felt sympathy towards the man in the morning but hatred towards him in the evening. The minister informed the wood-cutter, "The king is planning to construct a new palace, for which he will require a large quantity of sandalwood. You do not have to wait for the king to die to sell your wood. You will be able to sell it for a high price within a few days."

The wood-cutter's eyes gleamed with joy. The minister explained that he was an adviser to the king and suggested that he should place his proposal before the king. The wood-cutter immediately agreed.

The following evening, when the king looked from his window and saw the wood-cutter pass by, he did not feel any hatred! He was amazed by this change in his feelings, and was convinced his minister must have done something remarkable to achieve such a miracle.

Is it possible for our thoughts and behavior towards people to change in one day? What is the connection between our thoughts and our relationships? The answer is very simple and can be provided by the science of thoughts.

It is important for everyone to understand the science of thoughts because this science is working all the time in everybody's life. Understanding it can usher in a major change in your relationships. Why do you feel love, hatred, fear, envy, and so forth in your relationships? The science of thoughts has the answer.

Connection between man and thoughts

The connection between man and thoughts can be explained in four successive steps. At the first step, you need to understand the secret of thoughts. At the second step, you have to understand how to watch your thoughts. At the third step, you must awaken your awareness regarding your thoughts, and at the fourth step, you must understand an important rule of nature.

First Step: Secret of thoughts

The science of thoughts says that there is a continuous transmission of our thoughts outwards to the world, and a person about whom we are thinking also receives the vibrations of these thoughts. Even while we are fully engaged in work, the transmission and receipt of vibrations from thoughts continues. You can understand the secret of thoughts more deeply through the examples below.

1. You may have observed how children are attracted to those who feel a natural love for children. Why does this happen? Children are drawn to those people because their subconscious mind receives loving signals from them. If you compare an individual who has no interest in children with one who is fond of children, you will see that children are not drawn towards those who are disinterested in them.

2. While travelling in a bus or train, or standing in a queue, you may have experienced a sudden feeling of dislike or unfriendliness towards the person in front or next to you. The reason for these sudden feelings is the transmission of negative thoughts from that person.

3. Even animals receive such thought transmissions. You will have observed how intelligent dogs will follow around people who like dogs, but are wary of those who do not.

4. Some of your friends and relatives, despite their good behavior, may not always feel positively towards you. You catch these signals not by what they say but through your instinct for their thoughts. This tells us that relationships cannot be improved by superficial behavior. A new light in relationships can be brought about only through thoughts of love, compassion, and joy.

You will understand the secret from these examples that our thoughts alone are the reason for the success or failure of our relationships. If your social relations are good and strong, it is only due to your thoughts. If people do not seem to be close to you, this is also because of your thoughts.

Working on this secret of thoughts can be a very important step towards improving your relationships. To do so, you need to arouse feelings in your thoughts of love towards others. When looking at another person, say in your mind, "I like you because…" Here, many appropriate answers could appear in your mind such as: "You are always punctual… you manage everything in an orderly way… you behave lovingly with people… you are interested in learning and teaching… you always speak clearly… your language is polite… you are respectful to everyone… you are ready for any task… you always help people."

The above are just examples of how we should see good qualities in others, to give rise to respect, love, and liking in our minds towards each person.

Take advantage of the science of thoughts by learning the technique of changing your thoughts. This secret of thoughts is constantly operating, whether you believe in it or not. It is your responsibility to understand this secret and bring it into action. It is only due to our thoughts that some of our relationships are associated with negative feelings. With this understanding, let us learn to watch our thoughts at the next step.

Second Step: Watching thoughts

Every individual runs a factory in his brain, where thoughts are manufactured. Go and take a look into this factory in your brain and see what thoughts you are producing. You can sell only what you produce. Are you manufacturing positive, strong, coherent, focused, goal-oriented, loving, and happy thoughts, or are you producing revengeful thoughts? Always bear in mind that you cannot earn a good profit by producing goods of inferior quality.

If you are producing good and positive thoughts of well-being for all, then you will definitely gain the same several times over. However, if you are producing negative thoughts of hatred and malice, then you will get back similar negative results several times over. Let us remember this with the help of a small story.

A boy became fed up with his mother. He walked out of his house and climbed up a hill. Thinking of his mother, he shouted loudly at the hilltop, "I hate you!" This particular hilltop was surrounded by other hills, and whatever anyone shouted would echo back. The boy was not aware of this, so when he heard the thunderous echo, "I hate you! I hate you!" again and again, he got scared. He thought it was a demon who would kill him. Overcome by fear, he ran back home and told his mother about the demon. The mother understood what had happened. She told him, "Son, take me to that hill. I will set that demon right."

On reaching the hilltop, the mother told her son to shout out, "I love you." The boy obeyed. These words too echoed back: "I love you! I love you! I love you!" On hearing these multiple echoes of love, the boy was delighted. He wondered where the hateful demon had gone. The mother explained, "Son, whatever we give to nature, it returns the same to us many times over. If you desire love, then learn to give love. The demon is inside us. To kill it, we need to change our feelings. To change our feelings, we must change our thoughts. To change our thoughts, we must change our words. This is the proper and most effective way to ask for anything from nature."

By now, you may have some understanding of the power of thoughts, so let us return to the story of the king and the wood-cutter. Every morning, when the wood-cutter passed by the palace, he had no malicious thoughts about the king. He thought only of the cold and the hard work ahead of him to earn his living. The king's subconscious mind received the vibrations of the wood-cutter's thoughts. In response, the king's own thoughts turned to sympathy for the poor wood-cutter.

In the evening it was a different story. The same wood-cutter would return past the palace with his load of sandalwood. But now his thoughts were not of sadness but of how much he would earn from his wood as soon as the king died. This would bring an end to his family's poverty.

Even though the wood-cutter never spoke directly with the king, his thoughts were transmitted by his subconscious mind. In response to the wood-cutter's thoughts, which longed for the king's death, the king experienced a feeling of hatred towards him.

When the minister went to the wood-cutter's house, he managed to change that man's thoughts, by saying, "Why think only of selling your wood for the king's funeral pyre when the king will pay you handsomely now for building his new palace?"

With this in mind, when the wood-cutter returned from the forest the next day he had no negative thoughts about the king at all. Instead, he was thinking, "My poverty is over thanks to the king; he is very rich and can give me a good price for the sandalwood to build his grand palace." Now, as the king watched the wood-cutter return home, the negative feelings in the king's mind for the wood-cutter also vanished.

Through this story, the secret unfolds of how the science of thoughts works. What you think about others has an effect on them and what they think about you has an effect on you. Understanding and responding to this science of thoughts is an opportunity for you to improve your relations. Take full advantage of this opportunity.

Third Step: Importance of awareness in thoughts

It is nature's law that man's brain can never remain unoccupied. It keeps thinking, something or the other, so that it is always busy. Day or night, wrong or right, happy or upset, good or bad, man's brain is always thinking. The nature of the raw material you supply to your brain factory determines what it produces. If you are aware, if you have a high level of consciousness, and if you want a good environment, then it is up to you to supply the raw material of good thoughts to your brain. Furthermore, when you generate good thoughts for others, undoubtedly these good thoughts will multiply many times and be returned to you.

In some relationships, you may ask the question, "This person harbors bad thoughts for me, so why should I maintain good thoughts for them?" No matter how others think, you must always keep good thoughts for them because the rule of life always operates through your thoughts. This rule of life returns to you the fruit of your thoughts. Understand this rule at the final step.

Fourth Step: Rule of life

The science of thoughts would be incomplete without understanding this rule of life as the final step. This rule is a law of nature, which you cannot refute or ignore. The rule of life says: *The seeds you sow are multiplied a thousand-fold and returned to you by nature.* This is life's habit or nature's nature.

Just as one little seed sown in the soil is capable of producing thousands of similar seeds, nature works in the same way with the thoughts sown by man. Without sowing seeds, you cannot receive your chosen fruit. When you happily sow seeds of the fruit you want, you get the desired fruit multiplied a thousand times. Therefore, if you desire good wishes, then wish well for others. If you desire love, give love to others. If you desire respect, then learn to respect others.

This is the irrefutable law of nature, which is constantly at work. Just think, if you sow seeds of malice, hatred, misconduct, and criticism, then what kind of fruits will you reap? If you want good fruits, always be alert towards your thoughts and pay attention to your thinking patterns. If your thinking pattern does not yield good results, change your thoughts at once. Change negative thoughts to positive thoughts.

You can also deliberately use positive words to change your thoughts. Repeat such words as: "I love people... I talk to people politely... Everyone likes me... I do not need to criticize anyone... People do my wishes willingly... Every individual has some good qualities... By seeing and appreciating their good qualities, I get their full support... I will always see good in people and praise it... Everyone is good and noble... I love people." In this manner, you can change the words in your mind and thereby your thoughts. This technique is very effective, especially when you feel incapable of changing your thoughts.

Have you ever considered why storms occur? According to meteorologists, a storm arises wherever there is a vacuum and a drop in pressure. Nature dislikes a vacuum. Hence to fill the vacuum, it sends winds rushing to that area. These strong winds we term as storms. Similarly, if you wish to receive a storm of good wishes, then understand this rule of life and do not be miserly in harboring positive thoughts. Create a vacuum around you by giving positive vibrations to others in the form of good wishes, love, and joy. In response, according to the rule of life, you will experience a storm of positive vibrations coming towards you from all directions.

If you find it difficult to appreciate or believe the above mentioned rule, then simply try to follow it as an experiment for a while. Do not accept it blindly. First practice it and then believe it. If you experiment with this rule for a month or two you will see its benefits, and you will understand that this rule of life for improving relations always operates.

28

If every friend, relative, and neighbor, and every president of the world prayed for one another, then all hatred between relations and nations would disappear.

HOW TO BUILD GOOD RELATIONS WITH PEOPLE

As is our perspective, our body language, and our prayer, so is our world

In order to bring new life into your relationships and to ensure good relations with others, a small piece of advice can be useful: "Change your outlook and look at a new world." Only by changing our outlook can we improve our relationships. We need not struggle all our life to change others. Let us look at our own perspective, assess it and if necessary change it.

Whatever color glasses we wear, the world appears to us to be of that same color. If we look at a person through yellow glasses, he will appear yellow and weak. We would want him to get a doctor's prescription. But you know who actually needs a new prescription; it is we who have to change our way of seeing.

Often, we waste a lot of time in trying to change others, whereas we should use this time to bring about changes in ourselves. We engage in trying to improve others and constantly look at their mistakes, whereas what we need is self-development. *If we change our spectacles (perspective), everything in the world will change at once.*

Now we must decide which glasses to put on to look at others. If we wear glasses that are crystal clear and transparent, then we will see things as they are. We would be able to see only the truth.

Novel ways to view relations

Various kinds of people appear in our life. Every person arouses different feelings in us. Based on these feelings, we decide how we must behave with that person. Our behavior with any individual depends on how many times we have met them and the incidents that took place at the time. If our meetings were positive occasions, then our behavior towards them is always positive. From such occasions, we create a mental image of that individual.

One thing all of us must have noticed is that few of us behave the same way with everyone. Even in our own case, we know that we do not behave the same with every person. And others do not behave in the same way with us as they do with other people. Every individual behaves differently towards each other. Someone behaves very well with us, but the next moment we find them behaving badly with someone else. Often, we find that the person we had high regard for is being criticized by others.

For example, negative thoughts may arise in the minds of some people when considering their boss. Some would prefer not to see their boss at all. But at the boss's home, the scenario could be quite different. Somebody may be anxiously waiting for him/her to return. The children may want to spend more time with their parent and may plead to take a leave from office and stay back with them.

Everyone appears to be different to different people because their role with each one is different. The boss at a workplace may also be a husband or wife to someone, or a father, mother, brother, sister, son or daughter to others. As the role of this person changes, so does their behavior. Hence, some will call them dearest, some rude or strict, some helpful, and some funny. The individual is the same, but the viewpoint from which we look at them determines how they appear to us. This means that our point of view is the determining factor.

Before forming an opinion about any person, ask yourself, "Is that person really as I think of them? Does everyone see them as I do, or is my view a misunderstanding or just a personal belief?" This single question can end the misery and confusion we experience due to the 'unusual' behavior of others towards us. Subsequently, we will be able to look at everyone not with prejudice but with a new outlook. If we change our outlook and negative feelings (dark glasses), the entire world will change for us before our eyes.

How to transform others through prayer

If you have positive thoughts about family members who stay with you, you will derive energy and enthusiasm from them. If your thoughts are negative, your energy will be drained. Negative thoughts suck out your enthusiasm.

Do you have negative thoughts for those you spend your lives with every day – your family or your colleagues at work? You must always remain alert to this if you want to bring harmony into your relationships. Every morning when you wake up, you must affirm in your mind, "Today, some people are going to be happy because of me. I am going to be instrumental in raising the level of consciousness of anyone who meets me today."

As are the thoughts running inside us, so is our body language. Our body language is easily understood by the subconscious mind of others and vice versa. Negative body language quickly creates tension, constriction, and dislike in other people. But positive body language attracts support from all. As soon as our thoughts change, our actions automatically change as well. This process occurs so subtly that we do not even realize it. Hence, in order to change your body language, change your thoughts and pray for others.

Pray for those you wish to transform. Pray for your boss, friend, neighbor, relative, and so forth along these lines: "May all their desires be fulfilled and may they achieve abundance in health and wealth. May they be filled with mental and physical peace every day. May they overflow with love and bliss."

Pray for your boss and you will see an immediate effect in your thoughts. When your thoughts change, your words change too, and so does your body language.

Your body language cannot be negative with someone for whom you pray every day; it will definitely transmit positive vibrations.

These vibrations are received by that person's subconscious mind. Consequently, they too start behaving in a positive manner.

Such miracles occur when you pray for everyone, and such miracles should occur. Be it your father or your boss, your husband or your wife, your neighbor or your mother-in-law, in every case, it is you who have to change first in order to change them. This change in you will take place by praying for all. By praying, you will find that people working with you change on their own. Their way of looking at you and speaking with you will also change.

If you are an employee and are frustrated with your boss, if you are a daughter-in-law and exasperated by your mother-in-law, if you are a good citizen and aggravated by your neighbor, if you are a student and annoyed by your teacher, or if you are a teacher and troubled by your students, in all such situations it is crucial to correct your body language through the power of your prayers. If your body language is faulty, it emits negative signals. If your body language is right, it can change the world.

If every being on Earth – whether an ordinary man or the President, rich or poor, friend or stranger – prays for others and changes their thoughts, then all hatred will vanish between relations and nations.

29

The relationship that changes us from within and transforms us — that is a Bright Relationship.

BUILD A RELATIONSHIP THAT WILL TRANSFORM YOU

The unconditional relationship of Guru and disciple

Certain relationships are formed unconsciously. We do not question our relationship with a brother or sister. Nor do many question such faiths as Hinduism or Islam or Christianity into which they may be born. These relationships are accepted without questioning the reason or aim behind their creation.

In the olden days, there existed a tradition of child marriages, in which children would be married off at a very young age. One of the belief underlying this custom was that if the husband–wife relationship was formed without real awareness, then thoughts of divorce would never arise in the couple's minds. If you have considered someone as your brother or your sister since childhood, then you will regard them as a brother or sister for life. This tradition of child marriage was created to enable a potentially unbreakable bond between the two young people. Such relationships, formed unconsciously, have their own advantages. However, every unconscious relationship can impact upon one's life only as much as an unconscious object can.

We feel that we have no choice in our blood relationships, but there are other relationships that we make consciously. These can be the modern relationship between husband and wife, or the relationships we make with friends. In these relations, husband and wife consider themselves to be bonded with each other and, similarly, so do close friends. That is why there is an understanding and a feeling of acceptance of each other in these relationships.

The relationship made with highest awareness changes you

In addition to relationships made in unawareness and those made with an awareness of mind, there is also a relationship which is made with the highest awareness. This is the relationship between Guru and disciple. It is a relationship that transforms you completely.

Other relationships do not change you, because you remain caught up in false beliefs and aspirations, and your relatives and friends aid you in that. They will join you in watching fantasy movies, recommend to you the latest fashion styles, advise you on home-life accessories, perhaps even help you earn an income, but certainly listen to your grumbles as they tell you theirs. These relationships support you in ego, greed, lust, anger, malice, and hatred, but they do not change you. Relationships made in unconsciousness, or consciousness, can support you even with love, but they do not transform you.

The love that is present in unconscious or conscious relationships is not unconditional, selfless, real love; it is based on conditions. Unconditional love simply cannot exist in these relationships because they are filled with such expectations and demands as: "I did so much for you, now you should do this for me." If these conditions are not satisfied, then problems begin to grow. The breakup of any relationship is proof that it was never actually formed in the true, unconditional sense.

The unconditional relationship

A relationship made with the highest awareness has no such expectations because it is the unconditional relationship of a Guru and a disciple. In other relations, people keep conditions. For example, if you fail to attend your family's or friends' wedding receptions you may find that they fail to attend your own. Even if you consider that you have an unconditional love for everyone, which transcends such arrangements, they will consider only your physical absence. No such conditions can be formed in a relationship made in the highest consciousness. In this relationship, if you are offered an invitation but fail to attend, then the relationship is not severed. No conditions are placed on you because the relationship with you is unconditional. There is no place for conditions in this relationship. Hence, in such a relationship, one changes unconditionally.

Blood relations begin with the body, relationships associated with feelings begin with the mind, but the relationship with our true guru begins with the highest awareness. In this relationship, we can completely transform ourselves, because it leads us to realize who we actually are, our reality. *The relationship that changes us from within, alters our outlook and attitude, and transforms us, that's a Bright Relationship.*

When we become human beings, our first relationship is created with our mother in the womb and this relationship can be called a relation of *samadhi.** Although we experience the state of samadhi in the womb, but in this state there is also ignorance. After we are born, the next type of relationship is that of blood – our father, brother, sister, uncle, aunt, and so on. The third type of relationship is one we make as a friend, in which we choose our friends or a spouse. The final relationship available to us is with a Guru, in which we can again attain the state of samadhi. This relationship has been called the highest and the best, because the devotee experiences samadhi in the wakeful state due to the master's grace. Because of this, the attraction between the master and the disciple is the highest.

Reason for attraction between the Guru and the disciple

Complete opposites will generate the maximum level of attraction. When an individual seeks the highest, and there is one who can endow the highest, the attraction between the two is the greatest.

In other relationships, even between givers and receivers, the attraction may be neither strong nor lasting. For example, there

---

* Samadhi is the fourth state beyond waking, dreaming, and deep sleep in which we abide in the timeless and spaceless state of being and experience the unlimited Self as our true nature.

is very little attraction between a seller of vegetables and someone buying them. The buyer can choose to buy vegetables from any vendor, and for each vendor there are many customers. Neither does every opposite attract. The thief may attract the policeman, but the thief runs away from the police!

However, when someone says, "I want the Final Truth for which we have come to Earth," then this is the highest wish. This explains why the relationship between the Guru and the disciple is described as that of the highest giver and the highest receiver.

The Truth seeker is the one who asks only for the Truth. There is no hesitation or resistance involved in making this request to the Guru, as opposed to in other relationships. In other relationships, when conflicts arise, people stop speaking to each other. Due to hesitation no one initiates a compromise, and due to ego no one relents. When misunderstandings are overcome and communication resumes, there is a realization that this freedom from anguish should have been sought long ago. The joy of togetherness was unnecessarily postponed.

The Guru is the greatest giver because until approached by a real devotee who genuinely seeks the Truth he is not eager to impart the Truth. The attraction generated between Guru and disciple, or the giver and the seeker of Truth, is an equal one. This is why the relationship has been regarded as the most important of relationships, or a Bright Relationship, and beyond all others. It takes a long time to fully understand this relationship. When, in time, one does understand it, one gets liberated from all sorrows and from the cosmic illusion or *maya*.

In the outer world, people are lost in the material attractions surrounding them. Material objects are constantly being advertised on the television and other media. Through these advertisements, the cosmic illusion tells you… "If you feel thirsty, do not drink water, have this soft drink, it will quench your thirst." When, in fact, the soft drink will enslave your thirst. The cosmic illusion never speaks the truth. Its transmission and propaganda continues non-stop through advertisements, Internet and movies. There is simply no break in its flow. People do not find these illusory attractions to be wrong. They have no hesitation in following them. The body–mind of man is easily lured by material illusions. This is due to the behaviors and habits that have firmly taken root in the body, and the manner in which the mind has been programmed since childhood. The Bright Relationship works to break this attraction and to save you from this cosmic illusion.

Let us understand the relationship between the Guru and the disciple through the example of Ramakrishna Paramhansa and Swami Vivekananda. What was the attraction between this enlightened mystic and his principle advocate and devotee? Swami Vivekananda was bent upon attaining the Truth. He would question everyone, "Have you seen God?" When he asked this of Ramakrishna, he was not answered with "Yes" or "No". Instead, Ramakrishna took Vivekananda by the neck and said, "Whether or not I have seen God is not something that can be told in words. Come, I will *show* you God." The necessary intensity of thirst had arisen in Swami Vivekananda. Once he met Ramakrishna, the greatest giver possessing the highest wisdom, the Truth began to manifest in Vivekananda's life. Similarly, there are examples of Dnyaneshwar and Nivruttinath, Mira and Rohidas, Guru Nanak and Guru Angad.

When thirst for the Ultimate Truth awakens within the devotee, then the Guru *has to* enter his life to impart the Ultimate Knowledge. On arrival of the Guru, the power of wisdom manifests in the disciple and divine devotion manifests in the devotee.

The Guru will make his disciple undergo certain preparations before imparting knowledge to him, just as the ground is prepared before sowing seeds. Seeds are never sown directly into the ground. If the ground is stony, the stones are first removed. Unwanted weeds that have sprouted up are pulled out. Then the soil is watered and softened. After this, it is ploughed to create receptive conditions. Only after this process is the ground ready for sowing seeds.

When you become receptive or ready for something, it has to come into your life. When someone complains, "I am unable to find a job," he should be asked, "Are you ready for a job?" The greater your preparation, the bigger the job you are bound to get. This is nature's law. Once you are prepared, no one can stop that job from coming to you. In the meantime, you need to prepare by increasing your capacity, concentration, qualities, and skills, and learning the art of time management. Learning all these essential requirements will make you properly receptive.

Recognize the Guru with your heart

The relationship between the Guru and the disciple is that of the heart. At first, recognition occurs through the intellect, but as understanding develops the relationship grows from the heart. The Guru must be recognized with the heart. When this takes place, all resistance is broken and all bondages start breaking at once.

Imagine a man walking along the street smoking a cigarette. A relative is approaching, whom he respects a lot. Initially, he does not recognize his relative from far off, and so he continues to smoke. But when his relative stands in front of him, he suddenly recognizes him and throws away the cigarette at once.

He throws away the cigarette because he has love and respect for this relative. If he had no respect, he would not bother to discard his cigarette. When respect, love, faith, and recognition increase in the relationship between Guru and disciple, all negative habits and tendencies are discarded.

Man lives a constricted life due to his weaknesses, desires and habits, and thus he loses his real identity. When he recognizes the Guru, his heart reopens for love. When his heart opens, he realizes that it has been closed. Some people only come to know at the time of their death that they had been breathing all along, yet had never paid attention to it. If you acquire knowledge from the Guru before dying, then you will realize that you never die.

30

*Awaken your faith
and it will release you from all worries.*

How to Build a Relationship with God
Creative ways to communicate with God

Conscious man's first relationship is with God. As soon as he wakes up, he acknowledges God and worships Him. If worship is performed without any awareness, it becomes mere ritual. This will not bring a new light in relationships. But if we are aware, we will ask ourself these questions: "What is the purpose of my worship? Which relationship am I trying to improve? What is the rift that has developed in the relationship between man and God? Which prayers must be offered in this relationship? How can this relationship be strengthened? Which wall of greed or attachment has formed in between? How can it be broken? How can unconditional love develop?"

If the relationship between man and God improves by working on answers to these questions, this will in turn improve other relations as well.

When the first person flew the very first kite in the sky, what was the intention? The only thought within must have been: to communicate with God. This was surely a very creative person. Communication with God takes place within, but external actions can help. Not everyone is easily able to converse with God within. The mind is easily distracted and wanders off. This is why certain rituals are made such as bathing, wearing particular clothes, lighting a lamp or a candle, sitting in a particular posture, adopting positions with the hands, and so forth. All these rituals are carried out to invoke certain feelings, which help us to concentrate our mind and communicate with God. God's voice is subtle, it cannot be easily heard; hence we fail to recognize that voice. We can communicate with God only when we concentrate our mind.

The person flying the kite wanted to convey the need to start a communication with God. With the belief that God was above, the kite was created and flown in the sky so as to get closer to God. This kite was man's first feedback to God. Kites of different colors, yellow, red, green, blue, and so on, are a way of conveying our different states to God. The kite indicates to God our prayers and desires.

What could be the smallest such prayer? It could be "Help". When a ship is foundering, or a friendship or relationship is falling apart, we are in need of help. If a ship is sinking, a distress flag is flown from the highest point or a flare is fired in the sky, which signifies "Help". Similarly, when a kite flies up, it is a signal to God that help is needed below.

A person flying a kite must have the faith that he is contacting God. This faith works wonders. The faith towards God, which lay dormant within the person who flew the first kite, was awakened with the belief, "I am communicating with God; I have a relationship with Him." This faith should awaken within everyone. External rituals have been created to help awaken this faith. The flying of a kite acknowledges this faith and symbolizes: "I have told God everything. My feedback has reached Him. Now, whatever has to happen will happen from Him, I can sit back without concerns." In this way, we have prayed, we have completed our job, our role has ended. Now all is in God's hands, it is His work and He will take care of it. Such faith can release you from all worries.

If festivals are instrumental in communicating with God and directing our prayers, then you must use them to your advantage. When everyone attains understanding of the Truth, then at such occasion as a harvest festival, people will not bring gifts as an investment for a better future but to celebrate the perfection of life's harvest here and now. They will not need to remind each other to behave and speak well on such occasions because they will recognize the same Self (Consciousness) that pervades us all. When understanding is lost we have to remind others of that within that joins together all relationships. Through ignorance, people feel they need a reason to openly smile or laugh. The Self inside us needs no reason to laugh.

• • •

You can send your opinion or feedback on this book to:
Tej Gyan Foundation, P.O. Box 25, Pimpri Colony,
Pimpri, Pune – 411017, Maharashtra, INDIA
Email: englishbooks@tejgyan.org

Epilogue

THE GOLDEN RULE

Relationship With Society: The Golden Rule
The real you

We all know that human beings are social creatures. We live within a social environment in which we interact with others and seek our own development. But how should we define this 'society' in which we live? Should we identify ourselves as members of a socio-economic class? Should we see ourselves as part of a religious or professional community? Society must be defined in greater terms than these. A highly evolved society can be formed only by a higher level of consciousness.

In this broader meaning of society, included is not only our family, but also our neighbors, relatives, boss, colleagues, friends, and supporters. If we want to improve our social relations, we must know the Golden Rule and start to apply it.

The Golden Rule has been imparted to us by Guru Nanak, Jesus Christ, Prophet Mohammed, Lord Krishna, the Buddha, Lord Mahavira, and all the realized saints, but with the passage of time its true meaning now fails to reach us. Some words have gone missing. Those missing words are the essential essence and wisdom of the Golden Rule. Today, it is essential that this lost wisdom is manifest again. If we get back that lost knowledge, then the Golden Rule will work in the right way.

The Golden Rule has been understood as: "Do to others what you would have them do to you," or "Behave with other people as you want them to behave with you." This can be understood by all. If you want people to speak to you respectfully, you must give respect to them. If you want people to listen to you, you need to listen to them. If you want people to help you, you should also start helping other people. This seems quite simple and logical. But there is a missing link and because of this people do not get the results they expect. The actual Golden Rule was and is:

Behave with people as you want them to behave with you – the **real** *you.*

Let us understand what this statement implies. If you behave with others considering them as bodies then you will receive no less in return. But after knowing your true self, if you look at others in the same light, then the Golden Rule will start working. This rule is applicable for everybody, it is so beautiful, easy, and simple, but its true meaning has been lost.

To implement this rule, we first need the answers to the questions, "Who am I?" and "How should people behave with the real me?" Once we have recognized our true selves, then we can say, "Behave with me in this same way." Otherwise, if someone says, "You are very smart," we are delighted, and if they say, "You are foolish," we feel bad. This happens only because we have not recognized ourselves. If we have not yet understood ourselves by recognizing our essence – the unlimited, formless, blissful Self – then how can we understand others? Due to ignorance about the Golden Rule, we lead our lives always expecting something from others. If our expectations are met, we are happy, otherwise sorrow accompanies us all our lives.

When you understand your reality, you will be able to say, "I am not smart or foolish; I am not the body, the mind, or the intellect; I am not happy or sad; in fact, I am happiness itself." When you realize this, your behavior towards others will be with the same understanding. It will not make any difference to you whether the other person has this knowledge or not. Your response towards them will be with understanding, because you know who they actually are.

Behave with people as you want them to behave with you – the actual you. This means you should behave with an individual, knowing who they really are. If man is not the body, the mind, or the intellect, then who is speaking through him? When you realize the answer to this, then your behavior will always be correct.

After considering the Golden Rule, you may feel it is difficult to follow and that perhaps you may not be able to apply it. But once you begin to use this rule it will become increasingly easy to do so because it is your nature. Nobody needs to make an effort to live according to their own nature. The mind or the intellect may not accept the Golden Rule, but our heart knows it is the truth. This is because it touches our heart in some way. It is only when we work against our nature that we need to remind ourselves time and again of the Golden Rule.

Up until now, we have thought a lot about what we are not, but today we must think about who we really are.* When our ignorance vanishes we will realize who we are, and we will then find it easy to live by the Golden Rule. By following this rule in your relationships, your relations will become warm and loving, your behavior will be respectful towards one and all, and you will earn everyone's cooperation.

The Golden Rule has now been revealed in its complete form: "Behave with others as you want them to behave with you – the real you." In this rule, the important words are 'the real you,' which had previously been lost. Once you come to know 'the real you,' you can attain Self Realization**. When you get established in that state, nothing will remain except celebration... the celebration and bliss of being.

---

* To know more about your true nature, you can read the books *Complete Meditation* and *The Source* by Sirshree.

**To attain Self Realization, you can participate in the Magic of Awakening Retreat conducted by Tej Gyan Foundation. You can read about it in the Appendix of this book. In this retreat you shall learn directly what is true spirituality and what is the Ultimate Truth.

APPENDIX

About Sirshree

Sirshree's spiritual quest, which began during his childhood, led him on a journey through various schools of thought and prevalent meditation practices. His overpowering desire to attain the Truth made him relinquish his teaching profession. After a long period of contemplation on the truth of life, his spiritual quest culminated in the attainment of the ultimate truth. Since then, over the last two decades, he has dedicated his life toward elevating mass consciousness and making spiritual pursuit simple and accessible to all.

Sirshree espouses, **"All paths that lead to the truth begin differently, but culminate at the same point – understanding. Understanding is complete in itself. Listening to this understanding is enough to attain the truth."**

Sirshree has delivered more than 3000 discourses that throw light on this understanding, simplify various aspects of life and unravel missing links in spirituality. He delivers the understanding in casual contemporary language by weaving profound aspects into analogies, parables and humor that provoke one to contemplate.

To make it possible for people from all walks of life to directly experience this understanding, Sirshree has designed the *Maha Aasmani Param Gyan Shivir* – a retreat designed as a comprehensive system for imparting wisdom. This system for wisdom, which has been accredited with ISO 9001:2015 certification, has inspired thousands of seekers from all walks of life to progress on their journey of the Truth. This system makes the wisdom accessible to every human being, regardless of religion, caste, social strata, country or belief system.

Sirshree is the founder of Tej Gyan Foundation, a no-profit organization committed to raising mass consciousness with branches in India, the United States, Europe and Asia-Pacific. Sirshree's retreats have transformed the lives of thousands and his teachings have inspired various social initiatives for raising global consciousness.

His published work includes more than 100 books, some of which have been translated in more than 10 languages and published by leading publishers. Sirshree's books provide profound and practical reading on existential subjects like emotional maturity, harmony in relationships, developing self-belief, overcoming stress and anxiety, and dealing with the question of life-beyond-death, to name a few. His literature on core spirituality expounds the deeper meaning of self-realization and self-stabilization, unravelling missing links in the understanding of karma, wisdom, devotion, meditation and consciousness.

Various luminaries and celebrities like His Holiness the Dalai Lama, publishers Mr. Reid Tracy, Ms. Tami Simon and Yoga Master Dr. B. K. S. Iyengar have released Sirshree's books and lauded his work. "The Source" book series, authored by Sirshree, has sold over 10 million copies in 5 years. His book, "The Warrior's Mirror", published by Penguin, was featured in the Limca Book of Records for being released on the same day in 11 languages.

Tejgyan... The Road Ahead
What is Tejgyan?

Tejgyan is the wisdom of the existential truth, which is beyond duality. "Gyan" is a term commonly used for "knowledge". Tejgyan is the wisdom beyond knowledge and ignorance. It is understanding that arises from direct experience of the final truth. It is what sets us free from the limitations of the mind and opens us to our highest potential.

In today's world, there are people who feel disharmony and are desperately trying to achieve balance in an unpredictable life. Tejgyan helps them in harmonizing with their true nature, the Self, thereby restoring balance in all aspects of their lives.

And then, there are those who are successful, but feel a sense of emptiness within. Tejgyan provides them fulfilment and helps them to embark on a journey towards self-realization. There are others who feel lost and are seeking the meaning of life. Tejgyan helps them to realize the true purpose of human life.

All this is possible with Tejgyan due to a very simple reason. The experience of the ultimate truth (God or Pure consciousness) is always available. The direct experience of this truth is possible provided the right method is known. Tejgyan is that method, that understanding.

The understanding of Tejgyan makes it possible to lead a life of freedom from fear, worry, anger and stress. It helps in attaining physical vitality, emotional strength and stability, harmony in relationships, financial freedom and spiritual progress.

At Tej Gyan Foundation, Sirshree imparts this understanding through a System for Wisdom – a series of retreats that guides participants step by step towards realizing the true Self, being established in the experience of self-realization, and expressing its qualities. This system for wisdom has been accredited with the ISO 9001:2015 certification.

Maha Aasmani Param Gyan Shivir

"**Maha Aasmani Param Gyan Shivir**" is the flagship Self-realization retreat offered by Tej Gyan Foundation. The retreat is conducted in Hindi. The teachings of the retreat are non-denominational (secular).

This residential retreat is held for 3 to 5 days at the foundation's MaNaN Ashram amidst the glory of the mountains and the pristine beauty of nature. The Ashram is located at the outskirts of the city of Pune in India, and is well connected by air, road and rail. The retreat is also held at other centres of Tej Gyan Foundation across the world.

You can participate in this retreat to attain ageless wisdom through a unique System for Wisdom so that you can:

1. Discover "Who am I" through direct experience.

2. Learn to abide in pure consciousness while functioning in the world, allowing the qualities of consciousness like peace, love, joy, compassion, abundance and creativity to manifest.

3. Acquire simple tools to use in everyday life, which help quiet the chattering mind.

4. Get practical techniques to be in the present and connect to the source of all answers within (the inner guru).

5. Discover missing links in the practices of Meditation (*Dhyana*), Action (*Karma*), Wisdom (*Gyana*) and Devotion (*Bhakti*).

6. Understand the nature of your body-mind mechanism to attain freedom form its tendencies.

7. Learn practical methods to shift from mind-centered living to consciousness-centered living.

A Mini-retreat is also conducted, especially for teenagers (14 to 16 years of age) during summer and winter vacations.

To register for retreats, visit www.tejgyan.org, contact (+91) 9921008060, or email mail@tejgyan.com

About Tej Gyan Foundation

Tej Gyan Foundation (TGF) was established with the mission of creating a highly evolved society through all-round development of every individual that transforms all the facets of their lives. It is a non-profit organization, founded on the teachings of Sirshree.

The Foundation has received the ISO certification (ISO 9001:2015) for its system of imparting wisdom. It has centres all across India as well as in other countries. The motto of Tej Gyan Foundation is 'Happy Thoughts'.

At the core of the philosophy of Tejgyan is the Power of Acceptance. Acceptance has profound meaning and is at the core of our Being. It is Acceptance that brings forth true love, joy and peace.

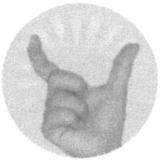

Symbol of Acceptance

The Symbol of Acceptance – shown above – is a representation of this truth. The symbol represents brackets. Whatever occurs in life falls within these brackets that signify acceptance of whatever is. Hence, this symbol forms the centerpiece of the Foundation's MaNaN Ashram.

The Foundation is creating a highly evolved society through:
- Tejgyan Programs (Retreats, YouTube Webcasts)
- Tejgyan Books and Apps
- Tejgyan Projects (Value education, Women empowerment, Peace initiatives)

The Foundation undertakes projects to elevate the level of consciousness among students, youth, women, senior citizens, teachers, doctors, leaders, professionals, corporate and Government organizations, police force, prisoners etc.

OTHER BOOKS BY SIRSHREE

ESSENCE OF DEVOTION
From Devotee to Divinity

There are two major paths to liberation: Knowledge (gyan) and Devotion (bhakti). You can attain liberation with knowledge, but there is the possibility of developing an ego of knowledge and thereby getting stuck in the illusion (maya) once again. Devotion is what will help you to remain established in the liberated state. Devotion gives you the power to easily overcome the obstacles to liberation—the mind, its ego and various tendencies. It adds joy and rythm to your journey towards divinity.

With the help of beautiful stories and examples, this book tells you everything about devotion; including what is devotion, its various aspects, its numerous benefits, as well as indications on how to develop devotion and reach the heights of devotion... where you realize that God and you are not two different entities—both are one!

ISBN : 978-81-84115-394-1

Total Pages : 184

WOW Publishings Pvt. Ltd.

ANSWERS THAT AWAKEN
Access the Source of Wisdom within You

Spirituality in its true form is neither an escape nor refuge. It's about reconnecting with our real self, realizing our hidden potential, preparing ourselves to deal with emerging situations and much, much more. Until we remove the blindfold of ignorance and understand the real truth about life and living, we'll continue to believe fallacies and get bogged down by existential dilemmas. The truth of life lies in the art of being one with life – a truth that not only takes us forward in our spiritual quest, but also elevates our level of consciousness.

This book is a select compilation of profound answers that arise from the quintessence of wisdom. These answers unravel the deepest truths about life and living, which dissolve existential dilemmas and reveal the essence of spirituality.

ISBN : 978-81-8415-627-0

Total Pages : 72

WOW Publishings Pvt. Ltd.

Good News!

Maha Aasmani Param Gyan Retreat
is now also conducted ONLINE!

You can participate in the retreat from the convenience of your home. The retreat is conducted in 3 parts during weekends:

1. The Foundation Truth retreat

2. The Bright Responsibility retreat

3. The Maha Aasmani final retreat

For more details, please call: +91 9921008060, +91 9921008075

To register, visit: https://www.tejgyanglobal.org/mareg

Books can be delivered at your doorstep by registered post or courier. You can request the same through postal money order or pay by VPP. Please send the money order to either of the following two addresses:

WOW Publishings Pvt. Ltd.

1. Registered Office: E-4, Vaibhav Nagar, Near Tapovan Mandir, Pimpri, Pune - 411017.

2. Post Box No. 36, Pimpri Colony Post Office, Pimpri, Pune - 411017

Phone No: (+91) 9011013210 / 9623457873

You can also order your copy at the online store:

www.gethappythoughts.org

*Free Shipping plus 10% Discount on purchases above Rs. 500/-

For further details contact:

Tejgyan Global Foundation
Registered Office:

Happy Thoughts Building, Vikrant Complex, Near Tapovan Mandir, Pimpri, Pune 411017, Maharashtra, India.
Contact No: 020-27411240, 27412576
Email: mail@tejgyan.com

MaNaN Ashram:

Survey No. 43, Sanas Nagar, Nandoshi gaon, Kirkatwadi Phata, Sinhagad Road, Tal. Haveli, Dist. Pune 411024, Maharashtra, India.
Contact No: 992100 8060.

Hyderabad: 9885558100, Bangalore: 9880412588,

Delhi : 9891059875, Nashik: 9326967980, Mumbai: 9373440985

For accessing our unique 'System for Wisdom' from self-help to self-realization, please follow us on:

	Website Online Shopping/ Blog	www.tejgyan.org www.gethappythoughts.org
	Video Channel	www.youtube.com/tejgyan For Q&A videos: http://goo.gl/YA81DQ
	Social networking	www.facebook.com/tejgyan
	Social networking	www.twitter.com/sirshree
	Internet Radio	http://www.tejgyan.org/ internetradio.aspx

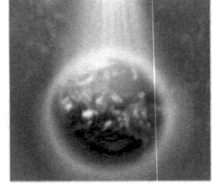

Pray for World Peace along with thousands of others every day at 09:09am and 09:09pm

Divine Light of Love, Bliss and Peace is Showering;
The Golden Light of Higher Consciousness is Rising;
All negativity on Earth is Dissolving;
Everyone is in Peace and Blissfully Shining;
O God, Gratitude for Everything!

www.ingramcontent.com/pod-product-compliance
Lightning Source LLC
LaVergne TN
LVHW040145080526
838202LV00042B/3035